# YALE HISTORICAL PUBLICATIONS

Leonard Woods Labaree · Editor

*MISCELLANY*

## XLVIII

PUBLISHED UNDER THE DIRECTION OF

THE DEPARTMENT OF HISTORY

FROM THE INCOME OF

THE FREDERICK JOHN KINGSBURY

MEMORIAL FUND

# FREE RELIGION

## *An American Faith*

BY

## STOW PERSONS

ASSISTANT PROFESSOR OF HISTORY

PRINCETON UNIVERSITY

NEW HAVEN

## YALE UNIVERSITY PRESS

LONDON · GEOFFREY CUMBERLEGE · OXFORD UNIVERSITY PRESS

1947

# PREFACE

ONE of the first duties of society, according to the novelist, Samuel Butler, is to pass such judgment upon its forebears as will consign them to that place in history, whether illustrious or notorious, which constitutes the true or vicarious existence after death that a thoroughly naturalistic outlook offers. The men and women of the Free Religious Association were products of the same influences that produced the delightful speculations of Butler, and were presumably as content as he to rest their case for immortality on the memory and pens of their descendants. Thus far it cannot be said that they have enjoyed a vigorous vicarious existence. To the best of my knowledge, my teachers, Professors Ralph Gabriel and Arthur Bestor, were the first to rescue Free Religion from complete obscurity, and subsequently others have observed that the matter deserved some attention. I do not pretend that my effort on behalf of the founders of Free Religion does whatever justice to their memory their acts may have earned for them. They exercised a certain amount of influence in respectable if limited circles, for which they have not received the credit that is their due. I have sought merely to open a case for them at the bar of history, and present some evidence, leaving to wiser men the ultimate judgment.

The librarians, who faithfully guard the tangible evidences of vicarious existence, have aided with their usual courtesies. I am particularly indebted to the staffs of the Yale, Harvard, and Princeton University libraries, and also to the Unitarian Historical Society and to the library of the American Congregational Association. Dr. E. Stanley Abbot and Mrs. Ralph G. Wells permitted me to use the papers of their father, Francis Ellingwood Abbot, and graciously shared much personal information. It is also a pleasure to acknowledge the kindly interest and material assistance extended by my colleagues in the Princeton University Program of Study in American Civilization. While Dorothy Reuss Persons has intercepted many errors and at least some infelicities in my manuscript, she cannot be held responsible for those that may remain.

*Princeton, N. J.*                                                   S. P.
  *August 15, 1946*

# CONTENTS

# I

## UNITARIAN ORTHODOXY

THE first week of April, 1865, was a time of unparalleled optimism for those fortunate enough to be living within the loyal portion of the United States. Lee's army, hemmed between Grant and Meade, and exhausted, was about to capitulate. Farther to the south, Joe Johnston, facing Sherman, would be able to hold out but a few days longer. Not only would one of the great wars of history be ended, but a great moral crusade would gain complete and dramatic vindication.

Five days before the surrender of General Lee at Appomattox on April 7 there assembled in All Souls Church, New York City, a National Convention of Unitarian Churches. In issuing the call for the meeting denominational leaders had urged Christians to drop controversies and mutual suspicions "and devote their united hearts and souls to the positive truth, the positive faith, and the positive work of the gospel of Jesus Christ!" In response to this appeal for the nationalization of a liberal Christian faith some three hundred and thirty-five delegates representing two hundred and two churches appeared.[1] In addition to promoting the positive aspects of the Christian religion the Convention was charged with the more practical task of organizing a National Conference of Unitarian Churches for the purpose of achieving effective denominational union.

With the eyes of the nation fixed upon the martial drama then drawing to a close, the Convention was presumably favored with no more attention than such occasions usually receive. For the delegates, however, the issues before the Convention were as momentous in their way as those facing the nation. In the opinion of many Unitarian leaders a radical minority was bent upon repudiating the entire Unitarian history and tradition, so that for the majority the issue appeared to be—Christianity or no Christianity. It was not that Unitarianism identified itself with Christianity in its

---

1. G. W. Cooke, *Unitarianism in America* (Boston, 1902), pp. 190–192. E. E. Hale, "The National Conference of Unitarian Churches," *The Christian Examiner,* 5 ser., XVI (May, 1865), 409–430.

entirety, but that it claimed to stand at the extreme left wing, beyond which one could not go while adhering to the Christian confession. To crush the radicals and secure denominational unity seemed nearly as important as the final defeat of the Confederacy.

The Unitarians were not a large group as American Protestant communions went, but they claimed for themselves an exceptionally distinguished history. Revolting from Congregationalist Calvinism at the beginning of the nineteenth century, they had won an almost complete victory over the latter in eastern Massachusetts. Entrenched on this promising soil Unitarianism identified itself with the "flowering of New England," and claimed its share of the spoils.² It had produced a Channing and a Parker, and if it had been unable to hold an Emerson, it could at least claim some negative credit in the matter. Yet, in spite of its eminent men and women, Unitarianism scarcely boasted a notable denominational history. The tradition of congregational independence as well as the social complacency of its members had proved an effective bar to efficient organization. The Berry Street Conference of Ministers had been formed by William Ellery Channing in 1820 to nourish the rudiments of denominational consciousness. Before the Civil War, however, the only national body representing Unitarianism was the American Unitarian Association, a missionary society composed of both lay and clerical members, formed in 1825.³ Other charitable and educational agencies were established in the Boston area,⁴ indications of a growing denominational consciousness, although G. W. Cooke, the historian of Unitarianism, admitted that

2. Minot Savage, one of the most influential liberal theologians of the later nineteenth century and a fairly learned man, compiled a list of great Unitarians for the edification of his congregation: among statesmen—the Adamses, Franklin, Jefferson, Webster, and Calhoun; literary men—Bryant, Longfellow, Whittier, Holmes, Lowell, Stedman; historians—Bancroft, Motley, Prescott, Sparks, Palfrey, Parkman, and Fiske; educators—Horace Mann and seven presidents of Harvard; scientists—Agassiz, Peirce, Bowditch, Draper; jurists—Marshall, Story, Parsons and Miller, and many more. M. J. Savage, *Our Unitarian Gospel* (Boston, 1898), pp. 8–9. The inclusion of some of these worthies may be excused as "religious license." Some Unitarians, in fact, have traced their lineage back to Ikhnaton.

3. O. B. Frothingham, *Boston Unitarianism, 1820–1850. A Study of the Life and Work of Nathaniel Langdon Frothingham* (New York and London, 1890), pp. 63–66. Cooke, *Unitarianism*, pp. 128–133, 140.

4. The Benevolent Fraternity of Churches, 1834; The Boston Port Society, 1829; The Seaman's Aid Society, 1832; The Young Men's Christian Union, 1851; The Society for the Relief of Aged and Destitute Clergymen, 1848. Frothingham, *Boston Unitarianism*, pp. 63–66.

a denomination in the strict sense did not exist before 1865.[5] The Western Unitarian Conference was organized at Cincinnati in 1852, but within a year it could count only nineteen affiliated churches in eleven states. One cause for the failure of the denomination to expand more rapidly was seen in its unwillingness to cultivate the home-missions field assiduously. This work devolved upon the American Unitarian Association, which in some years received as little as $7,000 for the purpose.[6] It was not until the middle of the century that the demand for denominational union and activity became strong.

Unitarian Christianity in the period 1820–1850 has been called by its historian "literary Unitarianism." [7] It was a mild form of evangelicalism, shorn of the vigor and somberness characteristic of the more orthodox formulations. Its lay members included the socially conservative New England aristocracy, the remnants of the old Federalism. This was especially true in eastern Massachusetts, where the oldest churches and the leading elements of the population had seceded from Congregationalism. The hardness of the old Calvinism, with its emphasis upon predestination and human depravity, had been softened, but otherwise Unitarians wished to remain as conservative as possible. They looked back upon their separation from Calvinist Congregationalism as a process of evolution, not of revolution, thus seeking to avoid the embarrassment which frequently plagues conservatives on the subject of their origin. Unfortunately, for Unitarian peace, however, the experiences of the past were not to be thus lightly assimilated in a process of harmonious growth. The virus of independent judgment in religious matters rooted itself firmly in the Unitarian body during the course of the controversy, and in later years the disease was to break out again and ravage the young denomination. But this was still in the future. Only a man so unusually perceptive as Channing could sense its presence, while facing the future with equanimity. In the meantime, Octavius Brooks Frothingham, who knew it intimately from his youth, declared literary Unitarianism to be more social than theological in its emphasis. It was a religion of good sense, stressing the virtues of private character on the assumption that with the creation of good men the regeneration of

5. Cooke, *Unitarianism*, pp. 158–159.
6. Hale, *Christian Examiner*, 5 ser., XVI, 414.
7. Frothingham, *Boston Unitarianism*, pp. 1–3.

society could be left to itself. It tended to avoid theological controversy and to concern itself with the refinement of culture and the cultivation of taste.[8]

Doctrinally, the Unitarian position probably was less an actual modification of the "New England theology" than it was a difference in emphasis. Aside from the great issue of Trinitarianism the differences were largely a matter of degree, although they seemed wide enough in those days of theological hair-splitting. In their conception of Deity the Unitarians were more inclined to emphasize the attributes of intelligence and love than of omnipotence and justice. They would agree with the orthodox Christians, however, upon the sufficiency and divine inspiration of the Scriptures. Both parties were convinced of the necessity for belief in the miracles to support the validity of the Christian revelation, although the Unitarians generally took the position that belief was not so much based upon miracle as it was further confirmed by it. Among the Unitarians there was little of that faith in the natural man characteristic of rationalist thinking.

In this respect William Ellery Channing was an isolated figure in his day. Channing had insisted as early as 1820 that "the ultimate reliance of a human being is and must be on his own mind." For in affirming the existence and attributes of God man must affirm the existence in himself of faculties capable of discerning those sublime qualities. "Nothing," said he, "is gained to piety by degrading human nature, for in the competency of this nature to know and judge of God, all piety has its foundation." [9] Channing had employed this argument in his attack upon the moral inadequacies of Calvinism. Appealing as it did to the rising humanitarian temper of the time, Channing's logic was too powerful for Orthodoxy, and his effective propagandistic work won him an enduring place in Unitarian annals.[10] Humanitarian as the implication of his doctrine was, Channing himself shrunk from putting it into practice. In his famous letter to Lydia Maria Child he confessed his instinctive distaste for that contemplation of evils which begets reform:

8. Frothingham, *Boston Unitarianism*, pp. 11–12. Moncure D. Conway, *Autobiography, Memories, and Experiences of Moncure Daniel Conway* (2 vols., Boston and New York, 1904), I, 170–171.

9. *The Works of William E. Channing, D.D.* (6 vols., Boston, 1841–1843), I, 226.

10. J. Haroutunian, *Piety versus Moralism: The Passing of the New England Theology* (New York, 1932), pp. 189–208.

My mind seeks the good, the perfect, the beautiful. It is a degree of torture to bring vividly to my apprehension what man is suffering from his own crimes, and from the wrongs and cruelty of his brother. . . . When the darkness is lighted up by moral greatness or beauty I can endure and even enjoy it. You see I am made of but poor material for a reformer. But on this very account the work is good for me. I need it . . . to save me from a refined selfishness, to give me force, disinterestedness, true dignity and elevation, to link me by a new faith to God, by a deeper love to my race, and to make me a blessing to the world.[11]

The fact that Channing could recognize and combat this tendency was proof enough of his moral greatness. The same factors of temperament, education, and socially conservative environment that shackled Channing operated to strengthen the passive piety of the Unitarian clergy in the generation following him, and most of them were unable to rise above their circumstances. The Reverend Nathaniel Langdon Frothingham, representative of literary Unitarianism in Boston, expressly repudiated the Channing position when he pessimistically declared that man, "poor worm!" was "approaching, as his last delusion, to the worship of himself." In general, the Unitarians believed that man was to be regenerated by supernatural means; certainly he was not to be trusted or admired in the natural state. The constitution of human society with all its infirmities, including poverty, crime, and oppression, was of a providential nature to be remedied only by the slow operation of spiritual influence stemming from personal virtue.[12] In the light of such principles it was not surprising that the Unitarians officially took little interest in humanitarian reform movements. Many Unitarian laymen and a few clergymen were exceptions to the rule, but generally these were liberals who retained the Unitarian name only because of the looseness of the denominational doctrinal and ecclesiastical bonds.[13]

11. Channing to Lydia M. Child, March 12, 1842. *The Letters of Lydia Maria Child. With a Biographical Introduction by John Greenleaf Whittier* (Boston, 1883), p. 46.

12. Frothingham, *Boston Unitarianism*, pp. 13, 44–49.

13. John Haynes Holmes, "Unitarianism and the Social Question," *The Unitarian*, n.s., III (Dec., 1908), 432. Dr. Holmes denies the contention of George Willis Cooke that Unitarianism did more in proportion to its numbers than any other religious body to promote the anti-slavery movement. Although it gave many leaders to the cause it did nothing as an organized religious body. He cites con-

The spirituality of Channing blossomed with some modifications in the following generation among the transcendental Unitarians. Not all of the transcendentalists left the church with Emerson, and those who remained carried Channing's doctrine of the dignity of human nature to its full development. They asserted that man's rational nature was a sufficient medium for the translation of God's revelation, thus undermining the unique position of the Scriptures.[14] The spreading of transcendentalist views within Unitarianism caused a further tightening of belts in conservative Unitarian circles. The Calvinist theologians were only too ready to identify transcendentalism with the entire Unitarian tradition, much to the disgust of the conservative Unitarians. The American Unitarian Association in 1853 committed itself officially to belief in the divine origin and authority of the religion of Jesus Christ through the miraculous interposition of God, as recorded by divine authority in the Gospels.[15] Thus the challenge of transcendentalism was met by conservative Unitarians with a new emphasis upon the significance of Jesus in the liberal theology, and with the reassertion of the place of that theology in the Christian tradition.

Characteristic of the Unitarian orthodoxy of this pre-Civil War period was the theology of Orville Dewey. Dewey had been brought up a Calvinist and had attended Andover Seminary before becoming a Unitarian. From 1821 to 1823 he was associated with Channing at the Federal Street Church in Boston. Other pastorates followed in New Bedford and New York City.[16] Dewey's chief purpose theologically was to show the correspondence between Unitarianism and the primitive Christianity of the Scriptures. He urged a return to the use of the terms "Father, Son, and Holy Ghost," atonement, regeneration, salvation, and election, as used in the Scriptures. Unitarians had tended to avoid them, because of the confusion resulting from orthodox Protestant constructions. Dewey's task was to restore them to their pristine definitions, and in so doing to trace the outlines of Unitarian Christianity.[17]

temporary evidence from S. J. May, Frothingham, Garrison, and Conway for instances of official hostility.

14. See Chapter II.

15. Cooke, *Unitarianism*, pp. 156–157.

16. Mary E. Dewey, Sketch of Dewey in S. A. Eliot, ed., *Heralds of a Liberal Faith* (3 vols., Boston, 1910), III, 84–90.

17. Orville Dewey, *Discourses and Reviews upon Questions in Controversial Theology and Practical Religion* (New York, 1868). The essays were written before 1846.

The Bible he asserted to be a divine communication, true in doctrine, historically authentic, recounting real miracles, glorious promises, and fearful threats. God the Father had sent His Son to mediate between God and man, although He should be considered as reconciling man to God, not God to man. Concerning the atonement there could be no question of the connection between Christ's suffering and our forgiveness; yet Dewey deprecated minute theological discussion of this doctrine, since the scriptural teaching on the subject was not precise enough to warrant it.[18] Unitarians, he insisted, believed in human depravity. There was no such thing as a righteous man; and the world on the whole was a very wicked one. This was not, strictly speaking, a natural state, for nature represented only capability, although Dewey conceded that the tendency was largely towards evil. Nevertheless, he insisted, Unitarians did not accept the pernicious Calvinist dogma of total depravity. There was some good in everyone. "Let us have some patience with human nature till it is less cruelly abused!" he exclaimed, with a gesture to Locke that revealed the sensationalist psychology underlying Unitarianism. The process of regeneration by which men were recovered from depravity was not a momentary transformation, but a slow process of change, in which God aided the individual. Election in the sense that the Scripture taught of God's infinite foreknowledge could not be denied, although this should not be warped into the stern fatalism of the Calvinists. Unitarians also believed in a future state of rewards and punishments, but here again the scriptural position was obscure, especially in regard to hell. That man should fear the future for his sins, however, was unquestionable. His was not to speculate, but to believe and fear.[19]

There was little or nothing in Dewey's teaching that had not found previous expression in various heresies throughout Christian history. To attach Unitarianism more closely to the Christian tradition was frankly his object. But Dewey and the main body of Unitarians following him found themselves under attack from both sides. The Congregationalist, Moses Stuart, looking out from the Calvinist stronghold on the hill at Andover, bitterly accused Dewey of gross deception in attempting to hide behind the time-honored formulae while resorting to the "artifice" of a new set of

18. Dewey, *Discourses*, pp. 7–16.
19. Dewey, *Discourses*, pp. 16–24, 114–117.

definitions.[20] On the other hand, from the point of view of the new transcendental "naturalism" which was working its way into Unitarianism, Dewey's position was distinctly reactionary. In reply to Theodore Parker's attacks upon the miracles Dewey insisted that to reject them and accept the supremacy of natural law meant atheism.[21] His own retreat from the budding rationalism of Channing to a mild form of evangelicalism was characteristic of the reaction of the main body of Unitarians to the new intuitive philosophy of the transcendentalists.

Strong as was the impulse of orthodox Unitarian thought to minimize its cleavage from the New England theology certain of its tendencies implied nothing less than the complete overthrow of the older religious attitudes. Without realizing it, the Unitarians adhered to views of man and his relationship to God that would lead many of their descendants to a purely ethical religion of duty. The transformation was to be a slow one, and the generation of literary Unitarianism traversed only the first step. In the controversy with the Calvinists the Unitarians had stigmatized the traditional complementary conceptions of God's justice and man's utter depravity as morally outrageous. Channing implemented the attack by demonstrating that the Calvinist view constituted a positive impediment to moral endeavor.[22] For many Unitarians, this was enough to demolish the ancient structure of theological doctrines concerning man, his nature, and his chances of salvation, and to require a new set of definitions consistent with moral freedom and a reasonably complacent view of the human situation. Channing was the obvious theologian to formulate the new position had he been temperamentally suited to the task. Like the transcendentalists, however, he had a strong distaste for definitions in the service of denominationalism, and so the duty passed to lesser men, of whom Orville Dewey was representative.

In placing new emphasis upon God's love and holiness the Unitarians were sounding the characteristic note of nineteenth-century evangelical Protestantism. Most of them were not prepared to follow all the way with Channing when the latter boldly proclaimed the excellence of man's moral nature to be the chief assurance of the benign intentions of deity. Ezra Stiles Gannett,

20. Moses Stuart, *Miscellanies* (Andover, Mass., 1846), pp. 205–206, quoted in Dewey, *Discourses*, pp. 54–56.

21. Dewey, *Discourses*, pp. 231–235.

22. W. E. Channing, "The Moral Argument Against Calvinism," *Works*, I, 217–241.

Channing's colleague and successor at Federal Street, listened with unconcealed alarm as his distinguished associate announced from the pulpit that the glory of Christianity consisted in the harmony of its teachings with the truths of reason and nature rather than in any peculiar doctrines of its own. To the younger man this smacked of pantheism.[23] A majority of the Unitarians preferred to follow the lead of the elder Henry Ware, who had taught that man is possessed of a "uniform" moral nature endowed with will power for either good or evil.

The new doctrines of God's benevolence and man's free will suggested an inversion of the Calvinist drama of salvation. The Christian experience as recorded in the Gospels was now conceived essentially as an ethical process, in which man shared the center of the stage. Christ's sacrifice, the promise of redemption, and the charge of man's responsibility became precepts and stimulae to guide the steps of the sinner toward the light. The curtain was rung down upon the former vivid delineation of the omnipotent God whose glory was inadequately measured by man's sinfulness and insignificance. Spectators would now leave the drama chastened, perhaps, but upright and with firm tread, trusting in the guiding hand of the Father.

These ethical implications were given characteristic expression in a sermon by Henry W. Bellows, pastor of the same All Souls Church in New York where the Unitarian Conference was later to be organized.[24] Bellows drew his inspiration from the parable in which Christ likened the kingdom of heaven to the leaven that a woman hid in three measures of meal, until the whole was leavened. The parable implied that as the leaven was for the meal so was religion intended for man, rather than for the glory of God alone. It likewise indicated that religion should be valued for its effect upon spirit and character, leavening the whole of life with its influence. Properly conceived, religion "suffuses our nature with a tone, and color, and atmosphere, instead of occupying it with a special and precise sentiment. It penetrates it like a savor, instead of puncturing it like a knife." Thus although religion was to be valued for its effects upon character and conduct, the apparatus of religion itself, its doctrines, worship, and study, must be maintained in good order so that its effects might be achieved. Bellows

23. William C. Gannett, *Ezra Stiles Gannett* (Boston, 1875), p. 218.
24. Henry W. Bellows, *Restatements of Christian Doctrine in Twenty-five Sermons* (New York, 1860), pp. 146–166.

derided the popular notion of religious faith as an external or
independent means of salvation. The kingdom of heaven is within
us, God and Christ are to be found within the soul of man, and
heaven and hell are states of mind.[25] The way to salvation lay not
in "getting religion" according to some prescribed formula, but in
living a virtuous life.

Rather than concede the sovereignty of ethics, however, and
accept the stigma of naturalism that orthodox Christians professed
to discover in these views, Unitarians insisted upon their essential
Christianity, and attempted to draw a clear line between themselves
and those who carried the line of reasoning one step further. The
task was the more difficult because of the relatively daring use of
reason made by Unitarians in their defense of religion based on
revelation. The Scriptures on which their faith rested must be
approached in a reasonable and common-sense rather than dogmatic spirit. Christ's mission, the forgiveness of sins, and the reality of the hereafter were abundantly clear to all who read. The
authority of the Scriptures in these matters was indisputable. But
many of the commonly held dogmas of Protestantism found only
tenuous support in holy writ, and with respect to these, Unitarians
preferred to keep silent. Insisting that revelation must necessarily
be incorporated in written records, they freely admitted the difficulties of interpretation implicit in the situation. Bellows rejected
verbal inspiration when he concluded that "the proper use of the
Scriptures is this: to fill ourselves with the spirit of them; their
pure morality and exalted piety, their great and undisputed facts
and principles, their general drift and aim; and then, thus furnished, to allow our minds, in the formation of specific opinions,
the freest play, which our total general culture, knowledge of human nature, experience of life, acquaintance with philosophy and
the general illumination of the age, demand or inspire." [26]

Approached in this spirit the substance of revelation was found
by Andrew P. Peabody to be in fact entirely consistent with natural knowledge. Peabody derived the title for his discussion of
Christian revelation, *Christianity the Religion of Nature*,[27] from

25. E. S. Gannett announced it as the prevailing Unitarian view that hell was
conceived as the flames of passion and remorse within the soul of the sinner. W. C.
Gannett, *E. S. Gannett*, p. 123.

26. Bellows, *Restatements of Christian Doctrine*, p. 208.

27. Andrew P. Peabody, *Christianity the Religion of Nature* (Boston, 1864),
pp. 32–43.

a work by the eighteenth-century English deist, Tindal, *Christianity as Old as the Creation, or the Gospel a Republication of the Religion of Nature* (1730). Peabody acknowledged the debt with the observation that only a naturalistic treatment of the problem would satisfy the critical intelligences of his contemporaries. In the very nature of things, revelation, he insisted, must always commend itself to men's reason. In all probability, God had vouchsafed a series of revelations throughout human history, each one adapted to the mentality of the epoch. Christianity was but the latest, suited to the needs of the race in its adulthood. The Unitarian conception of Christianity as a religion both reasonable and timely was to prepare the way for a younger generation to whom reasonableness and timeliness were essential, but who would entertain grave doubts whether orthodox Unitarianism fulfilled these requirements.

In compromising between orthodox Protestantism and deism, pantheism, or naturalism Andrew P. Peabody attempted to fix the Unitarian position at the extreme left of the Christian fold. As Plummer Professor of Christian Morals and college preacher at Harvard, Peabody made a strenuous defense of conservative Unitarianism against the transcendentalist views that were acquiring so much prestige in eastern Massachusetts. It was a mistake, Peabody believed, to assume that Christianity was established by the revelation of God in Christ. Christianity was anterior to all revelation; it is in fact the constitutional law of the spiritual universe, established from the beginning of time. Revelation was merely the natural and necessary means of imparting knowledge of the law to man. Currently popular means of apprehending divine truth through intuition, reason, or the argument from design were all tragically inadequate to establish faith in the Christian deity. Pantheism, which Peabody asserted to be the characteristic religious attitude of the eighteenth and nineteenth centuries, had amply demonstrated its incapacity to sustain faith in the Christian truths, or even to prevent the gross immoralities that were exhibited by its best representatives in classical times. He warned the unwary that the lofty monotheism displayed by certain modern deists must be attributed to the influence of their Christian nurture rather than to the dubious character of their views. In sum, Peabody insisted that the natural or innate religious impulse merely paved the way for the Christian revelation, without which there were no grounds for faith in personal immortality or individual providence.[28] This criticism of pantheism was but a thinly veiled attack upon transcendental Unitarianism. Moreover, it involved definition, exclusion, and denial, the pale negations that Emerson celebrated, rather than joyous affirmation.

The Concord sage and his followers were not the only ones to express disappointment at these tendencies. The aging William Ellery Channing, who had little sympathy for transcendental Unitarianism,[29] nevertheless deplored the new orthodoxy crystallizing within the denomination. In 1841, the year before his death, he wrote to the leading English Unitarian, James Martineau: "Old Unitarianism must undergo important modifications or developments. Thus I have felt for years. . . . Its history is singular. It began as a protest against the rejection of reason,—against mental slavery. It pledged itself to progress as its life and end; but it has gradually grown stationary, and now we have a Unitarian Orthodoxy. Perhaps this is not to be wondered at or deplored, for all reforming bodies seem doomed to stop, in order to keep the ground, much or little, which they have gained. They become conservative, and out of them must spring new reformers, to be persecuted generally by the old." [30]

Coincidentally with the tightening of theological lines came a drive to strengthen Unitarian denominational bonds. The American Unitarian Association was composed of individual membership only, and a mere quarter or third of the Unitarian churches were represented in it. In the period just before and during the Civil War the Association sank to a low point in its activity.[31] During the war, however, the Unitarians were mustered behind the energetic leadership of Henry W. Bellows, the organizer of the Sanitary Commission, and they emerged from the conflict with a greatly increased sense of solidarity. Strengthened by the success

28. Peabody, *Christianity the Religion of Nature,* pp. 16, 29, 31, 53–54.

29. Channing approved Parker's faith in Christianity as universal and rooted in human nature. See the latter's famous sermon, "A Discourse of the Transient and Permanent in Christianity" (1841), in *The Critical and Miscellaneous Writings of Theodore Parker* (2nd ed., Boston, 1867), pp. 152–189. But he regretted that Parker no longer felt the necessity to rely upon miracle. To Channing, Christ without the miracles was a fable, and the more he knew of Christ the less was he able to dispense with Him. Elizabeth Peabody, *Reminiscences of Rev. William Ellery Channing, D.D.* (Boston, 1880), pp. 423–426.

30. *Memoir of William Ellery Channing, with Extracts from his Correspondence and Manuscripts* (3 vols., Boston, 1842), II, 399.

31. Cooke, *Unitarianism,* pp. 158–159.

of his charitable efforts Bellows plunged into the problem of denominational organization with all the energy of a chief-of-staff assembling an army corps. Late in 1864, when the American Unitarian Association proposed to raise $25,000 to promote the work of spiritual reconstruction, a layman suggested that $100,000 could be raised as easily. But what did the Association represent? Surely not the denomination as a whole. Moreover, its campaign would cut into similar appeals for funds in behalf of other denominational activities.[32] At this point Bellows entered the scene with the proposal that the Association appoint a committee to plan a convention to deal with the whole problem of denominational unity. Each church would be invited to send its pastor and two laymen as delegates, so that the entire denomination might be represented. Bellows and Edward Everett Hale held the "working oar." They well knew that much of the doctrinal variety and spiritual vitality that characterized the younger Unitarians was possible because of the looseness of denominational bonds, but they were determined to secure theological and ecclesiastical unity even if it meant cutting off the radical minority.[33]

To the orthodox Unitarians the theological situation within the denomination was rapidly approaching a crisis. The conflict over transcendentalism had involved one of the two major assumptions of Unitarianism, the right of freedom of inquiry. Parker and his followers had won a substantial victory in defense of this principle when they refused to be driven from the denomination, although many of their nominal colleagues severed all association with them. The transcendentalists themselves had felt justified in retaining the Unitarian name because they regarded their faith as essentially Christian in character, and had carefully confined their differences with Unitarian orthodoxy to the question of the sources of religious authority. As to the nature of the Christian dispensation itself they stood as one with the conservatives. But now during the war years a new threat to unity appeared. Younger transcendentalists, or radicals, as they preferred to call themselves, were graduating from Harvard into Unitarian pulpits where the dangerous doctrines of Parker were tempting them to explore beyond, into the nebulous areas of rationalistic theism. The radicals in turn insisted upon their denominational right of speculative freedom,

32. Hale, in the *Christian Examiner,* 5 ser., XVI (May, 1865), 416–419.
33. E. E. Hale, Jr., *Life and Letters of Edward Everett Hale* (2 vols., Boston, 1917), II, 12.

but it was becoming increasingly clear that new philosophical currents and historical attitudes might prevent them from remaining loyal to the traditional Unitarian version of the Christian confession. Under these circumstances it seemed as though Unitarianism were destined to suffer one of the schisms so characteristic of American Protestantism.

When the preparatory committee for the National Conference met in January 1865 it found that considerable dissatisfaction existed among conservatives, especially the laymen, with the transcendental and rational tendencies growing within the denomination. One layman hinted that much money could be raised if the Convention should pledge itself officially to Channing Unitarianism. This term was used, twenty years after the death of Channing, to signify a faith centered upon supernatural revelation in the unique figure of Christ, confirmed by miracles. It implied a repudiation both of the transcendentalism of Parker and his followers and of the newer radicalism based upon rational and empirical foundations. The committee felt it wiser, however, to take no doctrinal position in issuing its call, although it was generally understood that the Convention would formulate some definite symbol or expression of Christian belief about which the denomination should rally. Whether or not the call which the committee issued was intended to allay the fears of the radicals is uncertain, but it was couched in most liberal terms, speaking of the task of the "liberal faith" as the promotion of the "positive work of the gospel of Jesus Christ!" [34] The evidence is overwhelming that the managers of the Convention were determined to commit the denomination to a theological position satisfactory to the conservatives,[35] but the radicals did not seem to have noticed the signs in the sky, and they came to the Convention in high hopes.[36] Their optimism can be understood only when the liberal spirit of the call is set against the exclusive denominationalism that characterized the Protestant sects of the period.

The organizing ability that had distinguished Bellows' work with the Sanitary Commission was in evidence when the Convention assembled in New York in April. Governor Andrew of Mas-

34. *The Christian Register*, XLIV, no. 5, 18. Hale, in the *Christian Examiner*, 5 ser., XVI, 422.

35. Lydia M. Child, *Letters*, p. 189. *The Christian Register*, XLIV, no. 5, 18. Hale, *Life and Letters of E. E. Hale*, II, 12.

36. O. B. Frothingham, *The Unitarian Convention and the Times. A Palm Sunday Sermon.* (New York, 1865), p. 2.

sachusetts occupied the chair, and the program moved with the smoothness of a well-oiled machine. On the second day a committee dominated by Bellows presented a plan for the organization of a National Conference of Unitarian Churches. The proposed constitution stated that its members were disciples of "the Lord Jesus Christ," dedicated to the advancement of His kingdom.[37] Short as these phrases were, they were sufficiently offensive to the radicals to launch a struggle which culminated two years later with the virtual secession of several promising young men from the Unitarian denomination. The transcendentalists, speaking through David A. Wasson, Theodore Parker's successor at the Boston Music Hall, objected to the use of "the Lord Jesus Christ" because of the universally trinitarian implication which identified Christ with God. Although the transcendentalists were willing to admit the providential, if not the supernatural, leadership of Jesus, the source of their religious experience was found within the individual, and the application of the term Lord to any other than God was offensive to them.[38] The younger rationalists, of whom Edward C. Towne of Medford, Massachusetts, was the chief representative, found their religious credentials in the empirical fact of universal religious faith among men; and to pledge submission to Christ would be an act of sectarianism inconsistent with a wider fellowship.[39] For both groups the higher Biblical criticism and the new historical consciousness had destroyed the literally interpreted scriptural Christianity which they professed to see in the term "the Lord Jesus Christ."

In spite of these wide differences within the denomination, Bellows and the conservatives were determined to secure organization around a creed acceptable to the more wealthy and influential Unitarians. The details of the proceedings at All Souls Church were a warning to the transcendentalists and radicals who had heretofore enjoyed doctrinal freedom within the Unitarian communion. The Convention agreed that each speaker on the subject of the creed should be limited to fifteen minutes. After Wasson

37. Cooke, *Unitarianism*, p. 193. The *Report of the Convention of Unitarian Churches Held in New York, on the 5th and 6th of April, 1865, and of the Organization of the National Conference* (Boston, 1866) was the official summary, carefully expurgated to gloss over the conflicts which developed. Edward C. Towne, *Unitarian Fellowship and Liberty: A Letter to Rev. Henry W. Bellows, D.D.* (Cambridge, Mass., 1866), p. 6. Towne's pamphlet, bitterly hostile to the conservatives, contains the only detailed account of the Convention.

38. Towne, *Unitarian Fellowship*, pp. 8–9.

39. Towne, *Unitarian Fellowship*, pp. 12–13.

had voiced his protest the floor was obtained by C. C. Burleigh, the distinguished abolitionist, who maintained that no authority could be found in the Gospels for the concept of Jesus as the Messiah. With shocking directness he announced that properly translated the term "Lord" would shrink to a simple "Mister" Jesus Christ. Burleigh was an excellent representative of tendencies from which the majority was most anxious to disassociate itself. His abolitionism might be overlooked in the year of Appomattox, but he was also a champion of many other reforms including anti-Sabbatarianism, a by-product of ecclesiastical opposition to his reform activities. Worst of all, he was the founder of a non-sectarian radical congregation at Florence, Massachusetts, as the representative of which he was present in response to the liberal terms of the convention call. His unorthodox views were outwardly symbolized by his tattered and unkempt appearance. On the technical ground that Mr. Burleigh represented no recognized church, he was excitedly declared to be out of order. Tempers flared, one layman declaring his distaste for uniting with "rag, tag, and bobtail." It was bad enough to face rebellion by young radicals from Harvard College; these interlopers were too much. James Freeman Clarke, always the peacemaker, suggested that the name of the Conference be changed to Unitarian and *Independent* Churches. Dr. Bellows promptly brushed aside the motion as out of order, although he had no parliamentary privilege to make such a declaration.

E. C. Towne was then recognized by the chair, but before he could speak United States Representative T. D. Eliot, of Massachusetts, interrupted to move that the speeches be limited to five minutes. Towne appealed to the chair for his rights, and was sustained, although the chairman ruled Eliot's motion out of order not because the Congressman did not have the floor, but because his motion was not in amendment to the question of the creed then before the house. Eliot, without even rising, immediately moved that the question before the Convention be tabled. The motion was put and carried. He then moved that the debate be limited to five minutes for each speaker. This motion was also put and carried. Throughout the deliberate disorder Towne retained the floor, with what feelings may be imagined. When finally allowed to speak he was permitted five minutes only.[40] Before the debate had lasted an hour Eliot moved the previous question, and the

40. Towne, *Unitarian Fellowship*, pp. 8–12.

objectionable phrase was adopted by a sizable majority. Eliot, who appeared to be the mouthpiece of the Convention managers, again resorted to high-handed parliamentary tactics to cut off debate when the issue was revived later in the day.[41]

Sitting in the balcony and taking no part in the proceedings were two young clergymen who had ample opportunity to observe the virtues and vices of organization. The sympathies of each were with the radicals, and the events of the day strengthened those sympathies into conviction. They had come to welcome the organization of the "Liberal Church of America," and were compelled to witness "the Spirit of Truth walking on toward Calvary alone." [42] Octavius Brooks Frothingham sadly walked up town and persuaded his Third Unitarian Society to change its name to the Independent Liberal Church. Francis Ellingwood Abbot, the other observer, journeyed back to his parish in Dover, New Hampshire, and tore up a sermon he had been writing in which he had set out to maintain that self-surrender to Christ was the necessary core of religion.

41. Towne, *Unitarian Fellowship,* pp. 16–17.
42. Frothingham, *The Unitarian Convention and the Times,* p. 2.

# THE BACKGROUND OF RELIGIOUS "RADICALISM"

"CALVINISM rushes to be Unitarianism, as Unitarianism rushes to be Naturalism," according to the Emersonian aphorism.[1] The Concord seer thus summed up one of the more important intellectual tendencies of the nineteenth century. He perhaps considered his own position to be that of naturalism, as the more lofty transcendentalists displayed sublime disregard for precise definition. Actually, however, transcendentalism stood midway between Unitarianism and the new "naturalism" which was to flower in post-Civil War, Darwinian America. The free religious movement, in which was represented some of the finest religious thinking produced by the new tendencies, traced its most important roots from Unitarianism through transcendentalism. Many of the leaders of the Free Religious Association, especially in its early years, were avowed transcendentalists, and that fact has led recent students to dismiss free religion as merely the final phase of transcendentalism.[2] Actually, a major intellectual revolution separated them.

Transcendentalism in America was a many-sided movement each aspect of which represented a revolt against reigning traditions of the day. As a religion it sprang from Unitarianism, declaiming with Emerson against the "pale negations" of its parent. The strident demand for affirmation in religion produced a Theodore Parker, whose task was to prune off the tentative assertions which Unitarians still permitted themselves to make. Starting from new assumptions Parker discarded the necessity of scriptural revelation, and planted Christianity on the indisputable facts of consciousness. Orthodox Unitarianism was based on what was then called "sensationalism," the Scripture rationalism of

1. E. W. Emerson and W. E. Forbes, ed., *The Journals of Ralph Waldo Emerson* (10 vols., Boston, 1909–1914), X, 9.

2. C. L. F. Gohdes, *The Periodicals of American Transcendentalism* (Durham, N. C., 1931), pp. 229–254. Gohdes includes *The Index*, the mouthpiece of free religion, among transcendentalist periodicals. In reality, Francis Abbot, its editor and founder, had little intellectual sympathy for the transcendentalists, or they for him.

Locke and Paley.[3] It also retained as a heritage from its struggle
with Protestant orthodoxy the principle of intellectual freedom
for the individual. Like the affirmation of the right of revolution
in early American political life, the latter principle soon came to
be more honored in the breach than in the observance, as new ideas
undermined the positive foundations of Unitarianism. The ability
to reconcile rationalistic freedom of speculation with authoritarian dogma had been a lost art in New England since the days of
Edwards, and the Unitarians tended to emphasize dogma at the
expense of freedom. When Mr. Emerson enunciated his transcendentalist doctrines before the Harvard Divinity School they
cut the ground from beneath the Scriptures. The Unitarians, with
Andrews Norton at their head, denounced the new ideas as "the
latest form of infidelity." The orthodox Congregationalists had
predicted just such a fate for Unitarianism, which made the pill
even more bitter for the conservative Unitarians to swallow.[4]

Transcendentalism came to America through English and
French channels, and was embraced by clergymen concerned to
save their fundamental theistic assumptions from scepticism on
the one hand and spiritual sterility on the other. Consequently
American transcendentalism differed markedly from the German
original. Although Emerson and George Ripley were unable to
reconcile their views with the established ecclesiastical forms and
so resigned their pulpits, a majority of their disciples did not
find that necessary. Parker's refusal under pressure to renounce
the Unitarian name won for transcendentalism the right to a
place in the denominational fold. By 1860 a strong transcendentalist group was entrenched in a Christian communion, denying
the external evidences of revelation supported by miracle, but
finding more than adequate assurance of God's existence and of
His moral attributes within the human mind itself.

Thought was accelerating rapidly in these years, to use Henry
Adams' figure, and while most Unitarian or orthodox Protestant
believers of the decade preceding the Civil War considered the
transcendentalist little more than an infidel, in the light of post-
War developments the position of Parker, for instance, would

3. O. B. Frothingham, *Transcendentalism in New England* (New York, 1876),
pp. 109–110. Merle Curti, "The Great Mr. Locke: America's Philosopher, 1783–
1861," *The Huntington Library Bulletin,* no. 11 (April, 1937), p. 115 and passim.
4. C. H. Faust, "The Background of the Unitarian Opposition to Transcendentalism," *Modern Philology,* XXXV (1937–1938), 297–324.

scarcely cause comment in liberal circles. It never occurred to
Parker to question his own belief in a personal and absolute God,
divinely ordained moral law, and personal immortality.[5] Yet,
within twenty years of his death many Americans who had been
his disciples would declare one or all of these ideas to be pious
fictions. Parker had been willing at first to accept even the New
Testament miracles as within the normal capacity of any man
wholly obedient to his mind, conscience, and heart. It was only
later, under the influence of the Tuebingen school of Biblical
criticism, that he rejected the miracles. Frothingham, who was
Parker's most devoted disciple until he went beyond his master,
supplemented these general religious affirmations by recalling the
older man's enthusiastic veneration of Jesus, his devotion to the
New Testament, prayers, meditations, and cultivation of humble-
ness and self-denial. It seemed to Frothingham that as Luther had
transferred the authority of the Christian creed from the Church
to the Bible, so Parker had transferred it from the Bible to the
soul.[6] With each change of base the Christian principles remained
unaltered. Freed from external encumbrances and firmly seated in
the soul of man as a fact of consciousness Christianity became the
absolute religion.

Considerable importance attached to Parker's concept of absolute religion. It bore the same relation to the intuitive religious
approach of transcendentalism as did natural religion to the rational thinking of the earlier deists. In either case these intuitive
or natural ideas contained the essence, and Christianity must
measure up at its peril. To be sure, it never occurred to Parker
that Christianity might *not* be the absolute religion, but the very
method of presenting the problem in such a form indicated the
degree of relativity that had crept unwittingly into liberal religious thinking. Parker's successors started from the same premises, and the problems of a new day forced them to conclude that
the bounds of Christianity fell far short of absolute limits. The
historian can see the history of free religion spread before him in
Parker's phrase twenty years before the Free Religious Association came into being.

The efforts to graft transcendentalism onto the Christian stock
had other important results for liberal church history. Tran-

5. Faust, *Modern Philology*, XXXV, 194–196, 313.
6. Frothingham, *Creed and Conduct* (New York, 1877), pp. 10–12.

scendentalism in America acquired from that application a
religious rather than a philosophical character. A certain mystical strain, so strongly marked in Emerson, characterized D. A.
Wasson, Samuel Johnson, and many other members of the group.
James Murdoch remarked upon this aspect of transcendental
thought in America by way of distinguishing it from the Kantian
version, which was concerned with practical philosophical problems.[7] The effect of this mysticism was to heighten the contrast
between the sensationalism dominant in the American mind of
the time and the extreme intuitionism of the transcendentalists.
The bitterness of the Unitarian attack upon this new "infidelity"
traced precisely to the willingness of the transcendentalists to
plunge into the elusive depths of personality not only to explain
the origin of knowledge and the source of subjective ideas but
even to substantiate moral liberty, duty, and religious truth.
Orthodox Unitarians believed the supposed religious instincts of
transcendentalism to be vague and without any guarantee of
verity. These instincts certainly varied widely among different
people, and if examined closely would probably turn out to be
not instincts at all, but rational deductions.[8] In reply to the demand of Henry Ware, Jr., that he set forth the proofs for his
assertion of innate religious feeling Emerson wrote calmly: "I
could not possibly give you one of the 'arguments' on which as you
cruelly hint any position of mine stands. For I do not know what
arguments mean in reference to any expression of a thought. I
delight in telling what I think; but, if you ask me how I dare say
so, or why it is so, I am the most helpless of mortal men." [9] Not
all of the transcendentalists shared this complacent contempt for
prevailing rationalistic methods in religious expression but their
faith in innate ideas rendered them all subject to suspicion. Believers in external guarantees for the principles of the moral and
spiritual life felt that the stability of society would be destroyed.[10]

Early in the nineteenth century the Divinity school at Cambridge had fallen into Unitarian hands. Transcendentalism in turn

7. H. G. Townsend, *Philosophical Ideas in the United States* (New York, 1934),
pp. 253–254. Frothingham, *Transcendentalism,* pp. 302–304.

8. W. C. Gannett, *E. S. Gannett,* pp. 222–233.

9. Ralph Rusk, ed., *The Letters of Ralph Waldo Emerson* (New York, 1939),
II, 167.

10. E. F. A. Goblet d'Alviella, *The Contemporary Evolution of Religious
Thought in England, America, and India,* trans. by J. Moden (New York, 1886),
pp. 184–185.

was placed squarely before it, under impeccable auspices, in the famous Divinity School Address of Emerson, in 1838. The Concord influence, bolstered by that of Parker after 1841, made itself felt in the student body almost immediately. Convers Francis even brought transcendentalism into the instruction when he joined the faculty in 1842. Francis was senior member of the "Transcendental Club." Although not an outspoken adherent, he used the intuitive method to bolster his Unitarian orthodoxy.[11] In the two decades before the Civil War many of the most promising students were converted to transcendentalism, becoming the free religionists and transcendentalists of the post-War period. O. B. Frothingham, John Weiss, Samuel Johnson, Thomas Wentworth Higginson, T. Starr King, and James Freeman Clarke all attended the School during those years. The Trustees were much disturbed at what one of them was pleased to call "the decline of moral earnestness." Since these young men certainly exhibited moral earnestness, it is safe to conclude that it was their views and not their earnestness that concerned the authorities.

By no means all of the students were immediately captivated with the new ideas. O. B. Frothingham was not, and Moncure D. Conway reported that none of the members of his class, 1854, was converted. Yet Conway noted that those untouched by transcendental religious doctrines were none the less infected with the social radicalism that pervaded the time. Reforms absorbed the attention of everyone: chiefly the anti-slavery movement, but also the peace, nonresistance, prison reform, and women's rights questions. Conway was convinced that this quickening sense of social obligation found its source in the spiritual individualism preached by transcendentalism.[12]

Another important contribution of transcendentalism to subsequent liberal religious thought resulted from its reëstablishment of contact with European and Asiatic philosophy and religion. By introducing and familiarizing literate Americans with the transcendentalist schools of Germany, France, and England, as well as with the mystic religions of the East, American transcendentalism was preparing the way for important new developments in religious thought. Parker's faith in the sufficiency of innate

11. Frothingham, *Transcendentalism*, pp. 353–354. J. W. Chadwick, "The Harvard Divinity School," *New England Magazine*, n.s., XI, no. 6 (Feb., 1895), 753.
12. M. D. Conway, *Autobiography, Memories, and Experiences of Moncure Daniel Conway* (2 vols., Boston and New York, 1904), I, 165–166, 169.

religious sense as the guarantor of religious values enabled his followers to cope with the trends of nineteenth-century thought unhampered by the necessity of reconciling natural knowledge with the dogmas of revelation. Armed with far more flexible intellectual equipment than that possessed by orthodox Christians, the transcendentalists welcomed the latest contributions to scientific and social thought with, if anything, a too glib assurance that their intuitive faith would be only further confirmed by the accumulation of natural knowledge. The theory of evolution, for instance, which presented such difficulties for orthodox theology, was welcomed by transcendental Christians without regard for its ultimate consequences for the transcendentalist method.

A more tangible contribution of transcendentalism growing out of the same cosmopolitan awareness of contemporary European and Asiatic thought was the awakening of interest in the comparative study of religions. Here was one of the major sources of free religious thinking. Parker's identification of the pure teaching of Jesus with absolute religion furnished the formula with which his followers approached the study of the great non-Christian faiths. Just as Parker had satisfied himself of the truth of Christ's message because it confirmed the absolute intuitions of the human soul, so his disciples based their faith on a universal religion that emerged in the great common affirmations found in all world religions. The one method had been intuitive, the other empirical. Although all of the free religious leaders of the post-Appomattox period displayed keen interest in the study of non-Christian religions, the works that best exemplify the importance of this interest for free religious thought are Samuel Johnson's three-volume *Oriental Religions and Their Relation to Universal Religion*,[13] and Thomas Wentworth Higginson's tract, *The Sympathy of Religions*.[14] The title of Johnson's study reveals the conviction of the younger transcendentalists that the true and abiding elements of each faith were identical, comprising a great universal religion. Higginson's tract, written in 1855, popularized this notion. It was the most widely distributed document of free religion.

The sympathy or agreement of religions, according to Higginson, indicated that in the last analysis there was but one religion for mankind, based upon faith in God, a future life, and obliga-

13. Vol. I, *India* (1872); II, *China* (1877); III, *Persia* (1885).
14. Free Religious Tracts, no. 3, n.d. Reprinted in *The Radical,* VIII (Feb., 1871), 1–23.

tions to one's fellow men. Beyond these fundamental affirmations similar doctrines of regeneration, predestination, atonement, and divine judgment were found in all great religions. Priesthoods, rituals, symbols, prophecies, and miracles displayed striking similarities to the objective observer. The sympathy of religions extended even to the loftiest of social virtues, to forgiveness of injuries, love for enemies, and the overcoming of evil with good. In addition to these universal elements, however, each particular religion required submission to its own messiah, whether he be Christ, Zoroaster, Buddha, or Mohammed. Thus each religion was seen to be "natural religion plus an individual name." In elaborating a universal faith the race had tended to deify its greatest teachers, and to pay to each its mutually exclusive homage.

These exclusive claims of inspiration maintained by the great religions were to Higginson their most repulsive feature. He could find no basis for the assertion of Andrew P. Peabody, for instance, that Christ's teaching was both unique in its time and still superior to all other religious doctrine. With extensive references to eastern and classical texts he demonstrated the essential identity of belief among the great religions. As a specific instance in which the Christian claim of exclusive inspiration reacted to its disadvantage he cited contemporary developments in India, where reputedly competent observers had noted the failure of Christianity to keep pace with the spread of Mohammedanism precisely because of the condescending attitude of superiority displayed by all too many Christian missionaries. Finally, Higginson attacked the most characteristic nineteenth-century claim of exclusive Christian inspiration. This claim rested upon the world dominance of Western civilization, which was attributed to the influence of Christianity. Higginson was content to observe that for the first thousand years of Christian history its alleged cultural superiority was far from self-evident; that the dominant cultural vitality of the West was actually a matter of the last four hundred years only, too brief a span to carry conviction. Once these provincial assumptions of unique inspiration were surmounted it would become apparent that the religion of the ages was natural religion, a universal expression of the human soul. Approached from this point of view natural religion was to become one of the important components of free religion.

The "secondary transcendental group"—Whitman's phrase[15]

15. Horace L. Traubel, *With Walt Whitman in Camden* (3 vols., Boston, 1906), I, 125–126.

—consisted largely of Unitarian clergymen converted by the eloquence of Emerson and Parker. Oldest among them was Cyrus A. Bartol, a graduate of Bowdoin and of the Harvard Divinity School in 1835. For fifty-two years he ministered to the needs of the historic West Church in Boston, nominally a Unitarian body, but actually contributing little of support or allegiance to the denomination. Dr. Bartol was among the first to perform the feat of combining transcendentalism and later more extreme radicalism with his Unitarian orthodoxy. This he did somewhat in the eclectic manner of Beecher, Robert Collyer, W. H. H. Murray, and other great preachers of the day, by emphasizing a large and tolerant humanitarianism shaped by the hand of a pronounced individuality. Bartol's opposition to the formation of the National Conference in 1865 expressed itself in a willingness to make his home a headquarters for the counter-organization of radicalism, which was to come shortly. His subsequent refusal to join with the radicals in forming this new organization, however, seemed to indicate that his rebellion stemmed more from distaste for denominational unity than from doctrinal conviction.[16]

An equally individualistic but more intellectual man was John Weiss, a Jewish Unitarian, also educated at Harvard. A witty "flame of fire" in his essays and occasional discourses, his theological positions were so finely drawn as to baffle all but the more learned of his brother clergymen. Weiss was for many years pastor of the Unitarian churches in Watertown, Massachusetts, and New Bedford.[17]

Rebelling against the orthodox reaction expressed in the Unitarian National Conference Weiss aided in the formation of the Free Religious Association, although he retained his status in the Unitarian denomination and served as a director of the American Unitarian Association. Weiss called his theological position "theistic naturalism." In the main it agreed with the views of the radical theists of his circle. But it was more spiritual, tenuous, and hazy on the points of religious affirmation, with doctrines of God and immortality scarcely calculated to comfort the distressed.[18] Here, in fact, was illustrated one of the great weaknesses of the free religious movement. It had no popularizers capable of stating

16. Charles G. Ames, in S. A. Eliot, ed., *Heralds of a Liberal Faith* (3 vols., Boston, 1910), III, 17–23.

17. Minot J. Savage, in Eliot, *Heralds,* III, 376–380.

18. O. B. Frothingham, in the *Unitarian Review and Religious Magazine,* XXIX (May, 1888), 418–421.

its position in a form that would appeal to the masses of people. In repudiating the irrational dogmas that clustered about the Christian tradition the radicals believed they were leading mankind from the age of childhood to that of manhood, as Francis Abbot expressed it. Yet the intellectual readjustment essential to maturity failed to take root in the popular mind. A new day was indeed dawning, but it was not the day envisioned by free religion. For this failure the over-sophistication of the free religionists was at least partially responsible.

The mystic of the radical group was Samuel Johnson, organizer of the Free Church of Lynn. Johnson entered Harvard from a conservative Unitarian background. Although he read the new transcendentalist literature of the American and European schools his faith in the old miraculous religion was first shaken by the "splendid, clear, truth-facing heathenism" of the classics.[19] From them he gained a sense of the beauty, order, and harmony of the universe, deriving unity and moral self-respect from experience by identifying the universe with the Infinite. His intimate friend, Samuel Longfellow, testified that Johnson had mystical experiences of personal union with the universe.[20] At the same time he welcomed the new scientific theories, especially the work of popularization carried on by E. L. Youmans, as substantiating his own belief in universal natural religion. A social radical, aiding the anti-slavery crusade by articles in the *Liberator* and the *Anti-Slavery Standard*, as well as advocating temperance and women's rights, Johnson was too dangerous for most congregations, and he preached around for seven years before being called in 1853 to the Unitarian church in Lynn. He would accept the call only upon condition that the society disband and reform itself as a Free Church. The Oxford Street Chapel built for him by his congregation boasted such novel features as free seats, voluntary subscription, and no confession save the motto: "Holiness and Progress, Prayer and Labor, God and Humanity." The congregation was never large, and the society disbanded with his resignation in 1870. An arch individualist, Johnson would never join the organizations whose motives he approved, including the Free Religious Association, although he contributed generously to the latter with lectures and essays.

19. Samuel Longfellow's memoir of Johnson, in the latter's *Lectures, Essays, and Sermons* (Boston, 1833), pp. 3–6.
20. Johnson, *Lectures*, pp. 14–15.

Social and religious radicalism were even more closely united in Thomas Wentworth Higginson.[21] The transcendental atmosphere that encircled the Harvard Yard, where he was brought up, caused Higginson to pass over a law career for the humanities, and to become an ardent disciple of the new spirituality. In Newburyport, his first parish, he preached transcendental Christianity and interested himself in the anti-slavery, temperance, peace, prison reform, women's rights, and labor movements. These activities cost him his pulpit, but gave him a fame which led to a call from the Worcester Free Church, a society newly organized in imitation of Parker's Twenty-eighth Congregational Society of Boston.[22] Like the Free Church of Lynn the Worcester group, or "Jerusalem Wildcats" as it was referred to locally, had no formal membership, communion, or specifically Christian character. Higginson compared it to Felix Adler's later Ethical Culture Societies, except that it retained the name of church and a slightly theistic tone. Like the other transcendentalists Higginson believed implicitly in the sufficiency of natural religion.

David A. Wasson represented the older transcendental spirituality in the free religious group. One of the few non-Harvard men among the radicals, he grew up under Calvinist influence in Brooksville, Maine. After attending Bowdoin College and the Bangor Theological Seminary, then a rigidly orthodox stronghold, he preached for a time to a Baptist society in Groveland, Massachusetts, near Lawrence. By a gradual modification of ideas he lost both his orthodoxy and his church, being forced out of the latter in 1852 by the local ministerial council.[23] The immediate formation of an independent society in Groveland won Wasson general recognition among the radicals. Ill health forced him to resign his charge in 1855, and he devoted the next ten years to travel and miscellaneous writing. In 1865 he was invited by the Twenty-eighth Congregational Society to fill Parker's old desk at the Music Hall. Poor health again forced him to retire after two years, although he had established himself as the society's favorite preacher after Parker.[24] Wasson's religious views represented a

21. Mary T. Higginson, *Thomas Wentworth Higginson, the Story of His Life* (Boston and New York, 1914), pp. 73–78.

22. T. W. Higginson, *Cheerful Yesterdays* (Boston and New York, 1898), pp. 77–131.

23. O. B. Frothingham's memoir of Wasson, in the latter's *Essays: Religious, Social, Political* (Boston, 1889), pp. 2–45.

24. Emerson to Charles Sumner, Dec. 8, 1864. Ralph Rusk, ed., *The Letters of Ralph Waldo Emerson* (6 vols., New York, 1939), V, 391.

more extreme form of Emersonian transcendentalism. Although he affirmed the sufficiency of the spiritual assurances found in the natural world he had a pronounced aversion to the "scientific theism" of Francis Abbot, believing that an analytical method swept the divineness out of life, leaving but a machine. His method was entirely intuitive and his definitions were as hazy as those of the traditional transcendentalists.

Most prominent among the early radicals and in many respects most representative of the free religious movement was Octavius Brooks Frothingham. Son of a distinguished Boston clergyman and related through his mother to Edward Everett and the Adams family, Frothingham represented the flower of the Boston aristocracy. He was educated at the Latin School and Harvard, graduating with the class of 1843. From earliest youth he felt himself destined for the ministry, and went on to the Divinity School as a matter of course.[25] There the issues of transcendentalism and Unitarian orthodoxy were being disputed anew by each class. After a careful consideration of the problems Frothingham took the conservative position, convinced that the teachings of Orville Dewey provided the most satisfactory solutions to the more urgent problems of the day. "Strauss was a horror," he later recalled; "Parker was a bugbear; Furness seemed an innovator; Emerson was a 'transcendentalist,' a term of immeasurable reproach." [26] That he accepted the conservative teachings because they seemed to assure the intellectual stability to which his early environment had accustomed him Frothingham later admitted. The subsequent conversion of conservatives of this type, of whom Frothingham was not the only example, was one of the impressive triumphs of the transcendentalist personality. The serenity, optimism, and humanitarianism exemplified by Emerson and his followers had, by imperceptible degrees, become formidable qualities that carried their own credentials.

Frothingham was converted to transcendentalism through the personal influence of Theodore Parker. In the course of routine pastoral work at the North Church in Salem, his first parish, he came into contact with the Music Hall preacher. Parker's persuasive views and wide interests started the younger man on the study of the new German critical scholarship of the Tuebingen school.

25. O. B. Frothingham, *Recollections and Impressions, 1822–1890* (New York, 1891), pp. 1–34.
26. Frothingham, *Recollections,* p. 34.

Under the influence of Baur and his students he restudied the gospels as historical documents with a dispassionate spirit that carried him to conclusions far more sceptical than the cautious opinions of the German scholars. Between 1847 and 1860 Frothingham passed from conservative Unitarianism to the transcendental Christianity of Parker, and finally, outstripping his master, went beyond the bounds of the Christian confession to a vague, non-Christian theism.[27] The good people of the North Church found themselves unable to keep pace with their growing pastor, and uneasiness inevitably developed. As a transcendentalist he began to make light of the traditional external assurances on which Unitarianism was based.[28] To make matters worse he became actively interested in the anti-slavery movement, a preoccupation most distasteful to his conservative Salem parishioners.[29] Finally, following a particularly touching rendition of a fugitive slave in Boston, the excited pastor, feeling many of his congregation to be in sympathy with the slave holder, took his cue from the ancient Church and refused to administer the communion.[30] Further service to the congregation became, of course, impossible, and a call to form a new Unitarian society in Jersey City was accepted with alacrity.

In later years Frothingham recalled his transcendentalist days with singular pleasure. They were shrouded in a joyous optimism never to be regained in the more sober times after the war. "In my own case," he recollected, "whatever of enthusiasm I may have had, whatever glow of hope for mankind, whatever ardor of anticipation for the future, whatever exhilaration of mind towards God, whatever elation in the presence of disbelief in the popular theology, may be fairly ascribed to this form of the ideal philosophy." When the transcendental phase gave way to "the faith of reason" Frothingham admitted that much of the old buoyant optimism was lost, although a greater surety replaced it.[31]

He never used the troublesome communion service again, and in other respects Frothingham continued along the road indicated by an avowed rationalism. He had never been able to capture Parker's facile assurance of the existence of God, individual im-

27. Frothingham, *Recollections*, pp. 57–59.
28. Frothingham, *Boston Unitarianism*, p. 250.
29. Frothingham, *Colonization* (New York, 1855) and *Speech before the American Anti-Slavery Society* (New York, 1856) display his strong stand on the moral issue.
30. Frothingham, *Recollections*, p. 46.
31. Frothingham, *Recollections*, pp. 136–138.

mortality, and the reality of the moral law from a mere examination of his own personality. At best he had been able to affirm that man possessed a spiritual nature which expressed exalted ideals clothed in the forms of temples and priesthoods. Appeal to the great religions for examples of universal spiritual and ethical precept became a favorite procedure.[32] Several years' study of contemporary European rationalist thought had destroyed the foundations of traditional belief, leaving Frothingham in a rarefied atmosphere that would, for instance, scarcely sustain the red blood in the veins of his metropolitan colleague, Mr. Beecher.[33] Little or nothing could be said with certainty about man's religion, but much about his religious nature; here was the spiritual basis of free religion.

Frothingham was not a great scholar, even within the premises of radicalism, but he performed a real service in calling the attention of the liberal American clergy to contemporary European Biblical criticism. The pages of the *Christian Examiner*, the scholarly journal of Unitarianism, bear witness to his industry during the 'fifties in introducing and discussing Baur and Renan, whose work he accepted at first reluctantly but with increasing assurance as the critical spirit grew upon him.[34]

Henry W. Bellows had urged Frothingham for the Jersey City post, and he now supported a movement to bring the young liberal to New York for the formation of a third Unitarian society. He did not suspect the extent of Frothingham's radicalism. The new society was organized in 1859, and rapidly developed into a "church of the unchurched." [35] The emotionalism of the war years easily carried over into contested fields outside of the political arena, and Frothingham was soon to be snubbed by his Unitarian colleagues, Bellows and Samuel Osgood. But a free and undenominational theism found a ready response among the metropolitan middle class. In ten years the congregation outgrew three church

32. Frothingham, *Recollections,* pp. 66–70, 59.

33. Frothingham, *The Weightier Matters of the Law; A Sermon* (New York, 1868), pp. 9–10.

34. The following articles from the *Christian Examiner* show the development of Frothingham's thought in the early years of his ministry: "The Christ of the Jews," 4 ser., XVI, 161–185 (Sept., 1851); "The Christ of the Gentiles," 4 ser., XVII, 1–35 (Jan., 1852); "Scientific Criticism of the New Testament," 4 ser., XXII, 94–122 (July, 1854); "Dr. Ferdinand Christian Baur," 5 ser., II, 1–39 (Jan., 1858); "Renan's Life of Jesus," 5 ser., XIII, 313–339 (Nov., 1863).

35. Frothingham, *Recollections,* pp. 63, 74, 102–103.

edifices and located itself in Lyric Hall, on Sixth Avenue. Six years later, in 1876, it was forced to move again to the Masonic Temple, which was forthwith dubbed the "Cave of Adullam" by the orthodox. Here Frothingham preached without pulpit and with the simplest of services to one of the largest congregations in the city.[36] With the formation of the National Conference of Unitarian Churches in 1865 the Third Society dropped its denominational connection and became the Independent Liberal Church.

If Frothingham was the leader and popularizer of the free religious movement in the early years Francis Ellingwood Abbot was its organizer and philosopher. The Abbots were an old New England family achieving in a less spectacular way intellectual distinction scarcely inferior to that of the Adamses and Lowells.[37] Francis Abbot attended the Latin School and Harvard, graduating from the latter in 1859 with highest honors. He supported himself in the meanwhile by teaching school for Frank B. Sanborn of Concord. While in college he had a "Christian experience" and joined the church, determining to devote his life to the Christian service. He prepared for the Unitarian ministry at Meadville Theological Seminary in Pennsylvania, where the controversy over transcendentalism was also dividing the student body.[38] Abbot emerged neither a transcendentalist nor an orthodox Unitarian, but a theist of a new "scientific" type. His first sermon, written at Meadville, September 24, 1862, stated the essence of a theology from which he varied only in detail during the following forty years.[39] God was held to be absolute in every sense. Human reason apprehended Him through a purely rational analysis of nature, which showed that He thinks logically. This was all safe enough, and in the best tradition, but Abbot carried the argument a step further. God and man have a common nature. "In ideal perfection, humanity contains no element which does not also belong to God. . . . To slander human nature, therefore, is to blaspheme God." Nature and humanity were full of God; and Christ, the perfect

36. G. H. Putnam, *Proceedings at a Reception in Honor of the Reverend Octavius Brooks Frothingham, April 22, 1879* (New York, 1879), pp. 15–19. The Ethical Culture Society, *Ethical Addresses,* ser. II, no. 10 (Dec., 1895), 117.

37. *The Unitarian Review and Religious Magazine,* XII (Nov., 1879), 552–556, in sketching the history of the Abbot family, observed that probably no family had exerted a finer influence on New England society.

38. Abbot, *Testimonials* (Privately printed. Boston, 1879), pp. 7–29. C. W. Wendte, *The Wider Fellowship* (2 vols., Boston, 1927), I, 168.

39. MS. sermon no. 1. Abbot Papers.

man, assumed God-like proportions. Abbot was no utilitarian. He held the moral law to be graven into the soul, with sin as real in relation to goodness as death is to life.[40] The Puritan temper, if not the Puritan theology, dominated his sermons in their uncompromising moral fervor. On the ethical side there was little to distinguish Abbot's discourses from those of any colonial divine.[41]

Two articles published in the *North American Review* in 1864 on "The Philosophy of Space and Time" and "The Conditioned and the Unconditioned" [42] gave Abbot a considerable philosophical reputation. C. S. Peirce, the founder of pragmatism, considered Abbot one of the strongest thinkers he had ever encountered,[43] while the Harvard professors of all persuasions, with the exception of Josiah Royce, echoed that opinion.[44] All the qualifications for a brilliant career in the ministry or in teaching Abbot possessed in abundance, and but for an iron-clad conscience which forbade any compromise with his radical convictions he would undoubtedly have achieved distinction. The bitterness of the struggle between free religion and Christian orthodoxy was nowhere more clearly displayed than in the persistent persecution that dogged Abbot throughout his career, turning it into one of the most colossal failures in American history.

After graduating from Meadville in 1863 Abbot preached around for a year before accepting a call from the Unitarian society of Dover, New Hampshire. His early preaching resembled transcendental Christianity of the Parker type, although actually his approach was far more rationalistic than Parker's. The agreement lay in their common conviction that unperverted Christianity was identical with absolute religion, the idea originally expounded by Parker. Jesus himself, both agreed, preached nothing but pure and universal religion. The observance of the Lord's Supper was justified, according to the younger preacher, but only as an act of inspiration for the participant. Immortality was likewise assured, at least tentatively, if one were willing to conceive of

40. MS. sermon no. 3 (1863). Abbot Papers.

41. The texts of the early sermons were customarily drawn from the Old Testament, and typical subjects were "The Bitterness of Sin," "The Antagonism of Life," "Sorrow," and "Jesus a Giver of Peace," all written in 1863. MSS. Abbot Papers.

42. *North American Review,* XCIX (Oct., Nov., 1864), 64–116, 402–448.

43. R. B. Perry, *The Thought and Character of William James* (2 vols., Boston, 1935), II, 431.

44. Abbot, *Testimonials,* pp. 26–39.

immortality as the fulfillment of human nature in terms analogous to the functioning of a physical organ. Man's earthly imperfection did not conceal his universal yearning for the great guarantee of immortality.[45] Presumably Abbot's parishioners were satisfied with the conclusions even though the reasoning might seem dubious or incomprehensible. It was evident that the preacher took his charge with the utmost seriousness, for no more earnest man ever entered the pulpit.

Certain tendencies in Abbot's preaching, however, began to alarm conservative members of the Dover congregation. He announced boldly that all truth, whether religious, scientific, philosophical, or historical was equally divine, and as such fell within the preacher's province. Any subject that might throw light on the destiny of man and his relation to the Infinite was proper matter for pulpit discourse.[46] This decree was followed by a sermon on "The Essence of Christianity," which must have impressed many as weak dilution rather than essence.[47] The traditional Christian idea of the fall and restoration of man through Christ must be rejected. Progress was the great law of history, for God was perpetually revealing Himself in a world that displayed the Divine Idea as it unfolded. Christianity itself had unquestionably experienced development through the centuries. Not that Jesus' teachings could be improved upon, explained the preacher, but that the world had been two thousand years in coming to a true understanding of them. He then traced the history of the Church from its authoritarian beginnings to its latest development in Unitarianism, where freedom was affirmed hesitantly, and achieved if at all at the expense of unity. The next step was to combine unity and freedom. Unity would be achieved by doing the will of the Father, while freedom would follow from the refusal to define Christianity as other than working the will of the Father. Everyone who should have Christ's spirit would be a Christian, be he Mahometan, Pagan, Deist, or Atheist. "There are but two parties in this world—those who live for self, and those who live for something higher and purer than self; and all such, whether this something be a personal God, or an impersonal law of duty, or the mere impulse and instinct of benevolence, share the spirit of Christ. Give them all the name of Christians, and your heartiest,

45. MS. sermons nos. 32 (Dec. 30, 1864) and 33 (Feb. 11, 1865). Abbot Papers.
46. MS. sermon no. 21 (Sept. 1, 1864). Abbot Papers.
47. MS. sermon no. 23 (Sept. 10, 1864). Abbot Papers.

holiest sympathies; make common cause with them, not in the
spirit of patronage, but of humility and Christian brotherhood."
No definition less broad would identify Christianity with absolute
religion, and Abbot would hear of no other.

In the light of such reasoning it is not difficult to understand the
opposition of the radicals when it was proposed that the National
Conference submit itself to "our Lord Jesus Christ." The connota-
tion was unmistakable. Unitarians were to be asked to confine their
intellectual activities to the limits of the Christian confession, and
there was as yet no tradition of freedom within those limits to
cushion the barriers. But this was still in the future, and in the
meanwhile the young preacher was grappling with the central
figure of the Christian drama. In June of 1864 he set down notes
for a sermon on "Faith in Christ." [48] Faith, according to the first
head of the argument, is self-surrender, the entrusting of self to
something out of self. Christ, who has identified his ideals with
himself, says, "trust in me"; and this self-surrender is the necessary core of religion. It does not mean the acceptance of intellectual dogmas or an historical narrative, but only adherence to
the spirit of Christ. Several problems immediately presented
themselves from this line of reasoning. Was it necessary that
Christ should have lived his life in order to produce its effect?
If the universe was the unrolling scroll of Deity could man
surrender himself to a prophet of the past, no matter how supreme?
How could one reconcile the self-surrender demanded by Christ
with the conviction that "self-reliance was God-reliance?" We do
not know what other questions occurred to Abbot, but he put away
the outline and the sermon was never written. When he returned
to the theme in July, 1865, the National Conference had met and
the die was cast.

Abbot had attended the Conference, but since his Christology
was as yet unsettled he had taken no part. The action of the majority gave a decisive turn to his thinking. The authority of
Jesus, he now informed his congregation, rested upon the truth of
His statements, and not that He had said them. Men had always
interpreted His precepts according to their reason, which was, in
fact, the essence of Christ's teaching. But His followers had not
been prepared for the new principle of the authority of individual
reason, and had set up an authority of Christ to replace that of

48. MS. outline for sermon no. 20 (June 25, 1864). Abbot Papers.

Moses.[49] The absolute standard established by Parker for the measurement of Christian dogmas had received full development in Abbot's assertion of the supremacy of private judgment. The sermons struck fire, Boston and Manchester papers reporting a movement on the part of certain elements in the congregation to dismiss the pastor. Abbot stood his ground, and reminded the dissatisfied parishioners that Christ Himself was something of a radical.[50] The majority, however, seem to have remained loyal, for Abbot retained his desk until 1868, when the development of his thought, rather than opposition from the society, forced him to decline to minister longer to a Christian congregation.

With the full development of his thought Abbot conceived of the universe as an infinitely intelligible and intelligent organism, in which each part, including man, participates in an evolutionary process of self-realization. His method of thought was rigorously logical, or scientific, as he preferred to call it, by way of distinguishing it from the common religious reliance upon revelation or upon innate religious feeling. Abbot was one of those rare philosophers who are moved by an intense desire to share their thought with the common run of men. The best years of his life were devoted to a popular exposition of his beliefs through preaching, lecturing, and writing. Under his editorship *The Index*, frankly popular in its appeal because of its forthright attack upon the Christian churches, maintained consistently high intellectual standards for the discussion of the current thought of the day. It was one of the major tragedies of Abbot's career that his conception of a free religion failed to incorporate itself in permanent institutions, although certain of his religious attitudes were to become current coin in subsequent liberal religious thinking. His chief contribution to free religion was to formulate the radical, or scientific, theism that shared with transcendentalism the dominant theological position within the free religious group. It was Abbot also who was to underline the differences of method and intellectual temper separating the two schools, thus contributing in considerable measure to the mutual dislike that was to weaken organized free religion.

The common bond uniting transcendentalist and scientific theist in the free religious movement was their rejection of dogmatic authority in religion, whether of scripture, creed, or au-

49. MS. sermons nos. 48 and 49 (July 15 and 29, 1865). Abbot Papers.
50. MS. sermon no. 49 (July 29, 1865). Abbot Papers.

thoritative revelation, in favor of a source of religious truth equally available to all men.[51] But beyond their repudiation of external fiat as the supreme religious authority major differences divided the two groups. Their conflicting views on the fundamental religious problems of the existence of God and the possibility of personal immortality posed a sufficiently rigorous test as to whether religious radicalism could find a basis of agreement sturdy enough to unite them in lasting fellowship. The transcendentalists professed unshakable faith in God and immortality through the assurance of immediate intuition or "higher reason." They entertained grave doubt whether any mere rational process of thought could provide these assurances, although their intuitive perceptions of the fundamental religious truths were for them facts as real and demonstrable as the brute facts that constituted the subject matter of natural science. Abbot observed that in religious terms this amounted to the assertion that a universal revelation had been vouchsafed to all men, apprehended through the "higher reason," of religious truths that transcended the sensuous or intellectual experience that was subject to rational analysis. Unfortunately, the transcendentalists were compelled to maintain their position in a day when many intelligent men displayed indifference or frank scepticism of the higher reason and the religious facts it supposedly substantiated. Consequently the transcendentalists concluded that these sceptics and atheists were somehow deformed in their lack of spiritual endowment or were at least undeveloped in this respect. Indeed, Abbot claimed to have observed among intuitionists an inevitable contempt for those who were unable to find assurance or authority in the higher reason. All of this amounted to the establishment of a modified religious dogmatism with degrees of spiritual excellence based upon the acceptance of an opinion that many intelligent men were unable to share. Those who, like Abbot, regarded moral conduct as the only external criterion of religious faith naturally found little in this respect to distinguish transcendentalism from the older religious orthodoxy.

The scientific school of free religion, on the other hand, took a frankly agnostic position on the matter. The existence of a large group of intelligent atheists in the mid-nineteenth century compelled scientific theists to admit that the possibility of God's

51. F. E. Abbot, "The Intuitional and Scientific Schools of Free Religion," *The Index*, II (April 15, 1871), 113–115.

existence and the chances of personal immortality were at best open questions. Whatever the ultimate answers, they would be arrived at by means of scientific investigation on the assumption that only the scientific method, formulating conclusions acceptable to the competently qualified authorities, could satisfy the critical intelligence. Abbot was the first to concede that in its existing state science was unprepared to solve religious problems. The scepticism of the age was in fact largely due to the disintegrating effects upon religious dogma of a corpus of scientific knowledge still confined to natural phenomena. But beyond physical science lay universal science, the investigation of the data of human experience in any chosen aspect according to the established scientific procedure of testing hypotheses arrived at inductively and deductively by reference to the relevant facts. The beginnings of scientific investigation of religion were already being made with studies of comparative religious beliefs and institutions or with critical analyses of religious records in their historical context. Tentative as these beginnings were they pointed to the day when scholars imbued with the scientific spirit would be prepared to supply definitive answers to the great questions of causation, freedom, purpose in organic development, moral sentiment, and religious affections.

Admitting that scientific investigation even of social problems, let alone these ultimate matters, was still in its infancy, Abbot deplored the tendency of certain pseudo-scientifically minded people to insist that only physical phenomena were the proper subject matter of science. Comtean positivism illustrated this tendency by attempting to exclude causal relationships from the sphere of investigation and thus reduce science to a mere exercise in classification. Abbot believed that the true implications of scientific method were exactly the opposite. No significant aspect of human experience was outside the realm of scientific inquiry. In the fulness of time, and as the world grew out of its infancy science and science alone would furnish the answers to the great questions that mankind is always asking. In the meantime, the individual could not be expected to ignore these questions while awaiting the final verdict. He must arrive at tentative conclusions as best he can, "in the spirit of truth, and in unflinching adherence to the laws of thought."

The differences between the two schools of free religion thus clearly delineated by Abbot in the early years of the movement indicated a profound diversity of intellectual temper that was never reconciled. The mystical strain in transcendentalism remained incomprehensible to the scientific school as well as to the great body of late nineteenth-century American intellectuals. As one by one they dropped into their graves the "secondary transcendentalists" took with them their serene confidence in possessing present and sufficient truth, leaving the field to rationalists who placed their faith in a hypothetical future in whose triumphs they could share only vicariously. Optimistic confidence in an ultimate mundane millennium combined with the daily restraint necessitated by suspension of judgment pending ultimate solutions became the hallmark of the rationalist mentality. But the full measure of these discrepancies was not taken at once by the rank and file of the two schools. Abbot himself partially concealed them by making no secret of his personal conviction that science would ultimately confirm his faith in God as a self-conscious and infinitely intelligent Being. For the moment, therefore, both groups gladly combined in attack upon the dogmas of revealed religion.

Individualistic though they were, these Unitarian radicals felt the need of organization, both for moral support and for the dissemination of their ideas. While Unitarian and secular journals were not closed to them the general tone of these periodicals was calculated to neutralize an occasional venture into radicalism.[52] The need was met with the establishment of a monthly religious journal, *The Radical*, in 1865. Sidney H. Morse of Boston, founder, editor, and publisher, was among the first to urge the radicals to break away from the Unitarian denomination after their failure to secure a liberal creed.[53] He disapproved, however, of a rival organization of radicalism on the idealistic ground that organization kills the spirit.[54] Morse had little sympathy for the rationalistic current that began to precipitate free religion from transcendental Christianity shortly after the War, with the re-

52. On occasion, radical contributions might even be subject to censorship. Abbot's attack in the *Christian Examiner* (5 ser., XVII, Sept., 1865, 157–174) upon the theology of Fredrick H. Hedge, the leading Unitarian transcendentalist, was arbitrarily modified by the editor, Joseph H. Allen, by means of an insertion in the first paragraph calculated to pull the sting of Abbot's criticism. Abbot's pencilled notation on the reprint preserved among the Abbot Papers.

53. *The Radical*, II (Nov., 1866), 182–186.

54. W. J. Potter, *The Free Religious Association: Its Twenty-five Years and Their Meaning* (Boston, 1892), pp. 9–11.

sult that the transcendentalists rallied to the *Radical,* while the rationalists found a new organ after 1870 in Abbot's *Index.*[55]

Another expression of dissatisfaction among many Bostonians with the existing ecclesiastical institutions was the formation in 1867 of the Chestnut Street, or Radical, Club. The Club was organized by the Reverend J. T. Sargent, a radical Unitarian who had lost his church by exchanging pulpits with Theodore Parker. Its meetings were held at Sargent's home in Chestnut Street.[56] Although designed to air progressive opinions, as the name implied, the Club actually extended hospitality to intellectual and religious leaders of many hues, from orthodox Unitarians to the arch radical, Abbot. Besides the older transcendentalists of the Emerson and Alcott vintage, with their disciples sketched in the preceding pages, regular and occasional attendants included such literary men as Whittier, Holmes, Henry James, F. B. Sanborn, and C. P. Cranch. Among Unitarian clergymen, Charles Carroll Everett, William H. Channing, Fredrick H. Hedge, and Samuel Longfellow frequently appeared. David A. Wells, Benjamin Peirce, and John Wesley Powell read scientific papers, while the philosophers Thomas Davidson, George Howison, and John Fiske lent gravity to the meetings. With the passing years the Club came increasingly to serve the general intellectual as well as religious needs of its members.[57] While membership was conveyed by invitation, the Club acquired a semi-public character through the full reports of its meetings carried in the New York *Tribune.* The reports were not entirely satisfactory, and Emerson, who objected to publicizing thoughts expressed in private, eventually withdrew from active participation.[58] In these and in other respects the Club failed to provide an adequate platform for the more aggressive radicals, who wanted an organization that might become the kernel of a crusade.

The decisive encounter between Unitarian orthodoxy and the radicals occurred at the First Annual Meeting of the National Conference of Unitarian Churches, held in Syracuse, October 10 and 11, 1866. In stifling discussion of the objectionable preamble

55. Wasson, *Essays,* p. 107. *The Radical* ceased publication in 1872.

56. Mrs. J. T. Sargent, *Sketches and Reminiscences of the Radical Club* (Boston, 1880). *The Index,* n.s. I (Jan. 6, 1881), 333–334.

57. Sargent, *Sketches,* Introduction.

58. Julia Ward Howe, *Reminiscences, 1819–1899* (Boston and New York, 1899), pp. 281–295.

the previous year Bellows had promised that the "Broad Church question" would be taken up at Syracuse, and the radicals prepared for it. Much discussion between the parties filled the intervening twelve months, with a feeling of tension increasing as the second conference approached.[59] Abbot arrived with a substitute preamble, which he printed and distributed to the members of the Conference in order to prevent the committee from shelving the matter. The alternative preamble asserted that "the object of Christianity is the universal diffusion of Love, Righteousness, and Truth"; nothing in the Christian position, truly stated, could possibly deny the right of private judgment, for "perfect freedom of thought is at once the right and duty of every human being"; Christianity, therefore, was defined as a practical ideal, rather than as theoretical dogma, and the basis of its organization should be "unity of spirit rather than uniformity of belief." [60]

On the motion of Dr. Hedge much of the second day was spent in discussion of the preamble. Abbot, Towne, and William J. Potter led the radicals, while Bellows and James Freeman Clarke "battled for the Lord." The conclusive argument was advanced by Clarke, who feared that removing the "Lordship of Jesus" from the preamble might be construed by the religious world as hauling down the Christian flag. When the matter came to a vote Abbot's amendment was rejected by a decisive majority. The Unitarians were determined to remain within the Christian fold, convinced that spiritual submission to Jesus in no way involved an infringement of individual liberty. Yet many of those who stood by the denomination did so with heavy hearts. The venerable Orville Dewey, who, more than any other, had codified the conservative Unitarian position, supported the radicals in principle while holding to his theology of miracle and inspiration. Although he was unwilling to give up his traditional theology, he believed the majority had been unreasonable in forcing even so vague a preamble on the radicals. Abbot had based his argument on the plea that where mere differences of opinion divided men otherwise in complete agreement concerning practical life and values their articles of union should stress the agreements and

59. *The Index,* VI (May 20, 1875), 230.

60. *Report of the Second Meeting of the National Conference of Unitarian and Other Christian Churches, Held in Syracuse, New York, October 10–11, 1866* (Boston, 1866), p. 20. The *Report* merely summarizes the proceedings and gives no inkling of the bitter struggle in progress.

ignore the differences. Only by such a method could Christianity and freedom be reconciled. Dewey went even beyond Abbot's demands in conceding the truth of some of the radical positions. He admitted that Christianity had its deepest roots in human nature, without which the Christian revelation would be meaningless. To the radical position he added only the conviction that Jesus strengthened and elevated man's naturally religious nature by a uniquely inspired life and teaching. Here was such a marked modification of the pre-Civil War Dewey that the theologian was obliged to assure Dr. Bellows that he had not gone over completely to the radicals.[61]

James Freeman Clarke, who had first won fame as a peacemaker by befriending Parker, now suggested that the name of the organization be changed to "The National Conference of Unitarian and Other Christian Churches" as a sop to the radicals, who might be persuaded to accept the preamble more gracefully if the title were broadened. The amendment was accepted by the Conference. It was apparent, however, that if allegiance to the Lordship of Jesus was to define the fellowship, it mattered little to the radicals how many other Christian churches were included. Abbot left the Conference convinced that Unitarianism had renounced forever its ancient principle of free inquiry, and that henceforward Christianity and freedom must be irreconcilable foes.[62]

61. Orville Dewey, *Autobiography and Letters* (Boston, 1883), pp. 293–295.
62. J. F. Clarke and F. E. Abbot, *The Battle of Syracuse. Two Essays.* (The Index Tracts. no. 15. Boston, 1884), p. 18.

# III

## THE FREE RELIGIOUS ASSOCIATION

THERE is coming on earth a spiritual as well as political democracy. Radicalism and not Unitarianism now represents throughout the whole world the advent of this new democratic civilization. . . . No political democracy can long endure, if indeed it can be at all established, while the religion of the country is in antagonism with it." Thus wrote Sidney Morse in *The Radical* for November, 1866,[1] after Unitarianism had repudiated its allegiance to unlimited freedom. The achievement of political democracy, Morse asserted, must be supplemented with a religious democracy which recognizes in all men the equal birthright of highest manhood. Yet, since no man is perfect, none will be called "Lord." In adhering to the supernatural lordship of Jesus Unitarianism represented spiritual monarchy, a religion of subjection. "A new spirit is swaying mankind today; a spirit of *wholeness*, which inspires these hitherto dull masses, and reveals to each an individual destiny." Triumphant democracy had demonstrated its political maturity over tremendous odds; it must now reap its heritage of religious freedom.

As he boarded the train at Syracuse to return to New Bedford the idea of a "spiritual anti-slavery society" occurred to William James Potter, an organization similar to the one whose labors had recently been crowned with success in the passage of the Thirteenth Amendment. The new society would dedicate itself to the emancipation of religion from the thraldom of irrational and traditional authorities.[2]

Potter was born of a Quaker family at South Dartmouth, Massachusetts. He graduated from Harvard in 1854, and after a year at the Divinity School there went to Germany in 1857, where he came into first-hand contact with the new Biblical studies by attending the lectures of Trendelenburg, Michelet, and Baur.[3] Re-

1. *The Radical,* II (Nov., 1866), 182–186.
2. W. J. Potter, *The Free Religious Association: Its Twenty-five Years and Their Meaning* (Boston, 1892), pp. 8–9.
3. Paul R. Frothingham, in S. A. Eliot, *Heralds,* III, 303–308. F. E. Abbot's biographical sketch of Potter, in the latter's *Lectures and Sermons* (Boston, 1895), pp. vi–xvii.

turning in 1859 he commenced a pastorate at the First Congregational (Unitarian) Society of New Bedford which lasted until 1892. Possibly because of his Quaker origin Potter had never placed strong reliance on the sensationalism of orthodox Unitarianism, and his studies in Germany stimulated his thinking in the radical direction.[4] By combining tact and mildness of character with his radicalism he was able to hold his congregation, leading them to extreme rationalistic theism. The spiritual antislavery society which he envisioned was realized in the Free Religious Association, and Potter was to be its principal driving force during the years of its greatest activity.

As the defeated minority journeyed back to Boston Potter revealed his idea to Abbot and Towne, who welcomed it eagerly, for it was now apparent that no refuge for religious radicalism was to be found within organized Unitarianism. They well knew that their struggle against nascent denominationalism had left them marked men in influential circles.[5] Nor were the younger radicals alone in their dissatisfaction with the new militant evangelicalism of the denomination. Several influential Boston clergymen of transcendentalist leanings were equally disturbed, both by the doctrinal tendencies in Unitarianism and by the aggressive measures to secure more efficient organization. The free religious revolt reflected traditional Boston independence as well as the new radical ideas.

Before the month was out, on a blustery afternoon in October, 1866, a little group of eight radicals gathered at the home of Cyrus A. Bartol, in Chestnut Street, on Beacon Hill, near the residence of the Reverend J. T. Sargent, where the Boston Radical Club was shortly to convene. The eight sat in a semi-circle about the open fire, with the young men, still flushed from the Battle of Syracuse, seated together in the middle. Bartol was ripe for revolt, and declared himself eager for organized protest or for a new denomination if necessary. To Samuel Johnson of Lynn, however, the predicament in which they found themselves could be explained as the inevitable consequence of ecclesiastical organization. Why invite the same result by forming a new denomination? Religious freedom could be promoted only by free institutions, the free church and its preacher, the free magazine,

4. Potter, *Lectures,* pp. xiii–xiv.
5. Potter, *The Free Religious Association,* pp. 8–9.

and the free lecture platform. Each man must do his work individually. Sidney H. Morse, editor of *The Radical,* already making his way as best he could alone, concurred in Johnson's sentiments. These two finally won over the older Bartol to their view. John Weiss, a director of the American Unitarian Association, although in complete sympathy with the radicals, was reluctant to break with the denomination. On the other hand, the younger men, Abbot, Towne, Potter, and Henry W. Brown, were determined that some kind of organization be formed outside of Unitarianism which should both assure the individual liberty of each member and provide a working basis of fellowship for objects which they held in common.[6]

A second meeting some weeks later revealed the same division of opinion. Assured by the older Unitarian individualists that sympathy, if not support, would be forthcoming, the radicals determined to test the sentiments of prominent nonconformists throughout the country. They first approached O. B. Frothingham, who welcomed the idea of a free religious organization, and consented to preside at a further conference, when plans should be laid for a public meeting. The acquisition of Frothingham was considered to be worth that of a thousand men.[7] Late that winter a third conference, still in the parlor of the hospitable Bartol, was attended by some twenty-five or thirty persons, most of whom were nominal Unitarian clergymen, besides a few laymen and laywomen, a couple of liberal Universalists, two or three Quakers, and several members of Parker's old Twenty-eighth Congregational Society. A draft of the constitution for a proposed Free Religious Association was presented by Abbot, Potter, and Towne, and discussed by the group.[8] The problems involved in constitution making were not simple. The organization must provide an adequate basis for expression of the religious convictions of its members, however radical they might be. It must guarantee to respect and protect those convictions no matter how seriously they might clash within the Association, for the whole protest against Unitarianism had turned about the defense of individual opinion. At the same time the new Association must be so formed as not to represent a definite break with Unitarianism, for to do

6. Potter, *The Free Religious Association,* pp. 9–11.
7. Potter, *The Free Religious Association,* p. 12.
8. F. E. Abbot, *Outlines of the Liberal Religious Situation.* (Free Church Tracts. no. 1. Tacoma, Wash., 1895), p. 25.

so would cost it much support, as well as contradict the very principle of freedom on which it was to be founded. Discussion of the plan lasted all day and into the evening, with sharp differences of opinion apparent.[9] A majority, however, pledged support to a new religious organization, appointing a committee to arrange for a public convention in Boston.

In the spring of 1867 religious and secular newspapers in New York and Boston carried announcements that "a Public Meeting, to consider the conditions, wants and prospects of Free Religion in America, will be held on Thursday, May 30, at 10 A.M., in Horticultural Hall, Boston. The following persons have been asked to address the meeting, and addresses may be expected from most of them: R. W. Emerson, John Weiss, Robert Dale Owen, William H. Furness, Lucretia Mott, Henry Blanchard, T. W. Higginson, D. A. Wasson, Isaac M. Wise, Oliver Johnson, F. E. Abbot, and Max Lilienthal."

On the morning of May 30 spacious Horticultural Hall was packed to the doors. Weiss, arriving at the front entrance, was unable to make his way to the platform. Emerson had expected a committee meeting, and was totally unprepared to deliver an address. The chairman, Frothingham, called the meeting to order with the announcement that a new religious revolt was taking place, which must be organized. In graceful periods he invited the assembly to join in the formation of a religious fellowship "independent of the regularly organized sects in Christendom." The idea had originated, he said, with the conviction that multitudes of truly devout people throughout the country were dissatisfied with the situation in their particular denominations. With this condition in mind the committee had invited dissident leaders from many groups to address the meeting. Speakers representing left-wing Unitarianism, progressive Universalism, Spiritualism, the Quakers, progressive Quakers, free religionists, liberal Jews, "come-outers," and scientific theists would address the meeting. Those in the audience with the stamina to remain to the end would be rewarded with a few words from "the great representative of the absolute in pure thought—Ralph Waldo Emerson." [10]

9. *The Index,* I (Jan. 1, 1870), 7–8.

10. *Report of Addresses at a Meeting Held in Boston, May 30, 1867, to Consider the Conditions, Wants, and Prospects of Free Religion in America. Together with the Constitution of the Free Religious Association there Organized* (Boston, 1867), pp. 3–7.

The scoffers, and there were doubtless plenty of them present, must have found considerable cause for derision in the morning's proceedings. The program had been planned to indicate the extensive dissatisfaction with denominationalism existing within even the less orthodox religious groups, and to explore the common convictions that might serve as a basis for union among these dissidents. Neither objective was fully realized. That there was deep discontent became evident enough, although little was said to indicate on what ground the radicals might erect a common platform. Nor had it been anticipated that the speakers would find as much to criticize in one another as in the established denominations. John Weiss was to have opened the meeting with an address calculated to indicate the basic evils of sectarianism, thus setting the pattern for the following speakers, many of whom were unknown quantities. Weiss, as we have seen, was caught in the crowded aisles, and when he did not appear on the platform Frothingham introduced the second speaker, the Reverend Henry Blanchard, a Universalist. Blanchard caught the spirit of the occasion only partially, and used his time to berate roundly the conservatives of his denomination. He pointed out that the same conflicting tendencies were at work in Universalism that have already been observed among the Unitarians. Both groups stemmed from the main body of Calvinism, and whereas the distinctive mark of early Unitarianism had been its denial of the Trinity, the Universalists had maintained the universal efficacy of Christ's atonement. From this single seed of heresy there sprouted ethical, humanitarian, and rationalist tendencies to form a characteristic Universalist liberalism. But while the liberals were moving toward rejection of the whole biblical drama of salvation, conservatives were pressing for closer denominational unity. Thus in 1867 the two denominational groups stood in much the same position. Blanchard, however, was not prepared to break new ground with the Unitarian radicals. He sympathized with their anti-denominationalism, but being unable to conceive of the Free Religious Association in other than broader denominational terms he doubted that any organization could be wide enough to embrace Christian liberals, non-Christians, and humanists.[11]

Lucretia Mott, the Quakeress, followed Blanchard, and chided

11. *Report of Addresses*, pp. 8–11.

him gently by pointing out that such sectarianism was precisely the evil the present assembly proposed to avoid. She welcomed the occasion as the manifestation of a new and non-sectarian practical piety consistent with the promise of religious freedom embodied in the American Constitution a century before.[12] Robert Dale Owen, of New Harmony, then urged the significance of the Spiritualist contribution to an age which demanded scientific proof for its belief in immortality. Weiss, who had by this time struggled through to the platform, dramatized the freedom of the occasion by ridiculing the pretensions of Spiritualism. Nevertheless, Weiss touched upon one of the essential characteristics of free religion when he insisted that the method of seeking religious truth, rather than the article of faith itself, constituted the new bond of unity. He would rely solely upon the intelligence to study the scientific movement of God's thought as it may be traced in nature, in history, and in the daily lives of men and women.[13]

The next speaker, Francis Abbot, insisted that faith in humanity was both the great affirmation of free religion and the sole basis for an unassailable theism. He reminded the audience that in the minds of its organizers free religion was not to be a Christian faith in the ordinary sense of a religion based upon the unique revelation of Christ, although it dedicated itself to ideals imperfectly realized by Christians. Acknowledging the best in Christianity, free religion transferred its loyalty from Christ to His principles: truth, righteousness, and love. The new faith in man made possible the reconciliation of religion and science. As a fact of human nature, the fact of aspiration and upward endeavor, religion revealed itself as a part of universal science; and it became one of the functions of science to interpret this fact with its implications for life as a whole. The new faith in man was to lead to the elevation and reform of society in all possible ways. Abbot closed his remarks with an impassioned plea for the new faith:

Brothers and sisters, we want to work for humanity. We have a new gospel to proclaim,—the gospel of religion and science, two in one,— the gospel of faith in man carried out to its extremest consequences, —the gospel of repose in the Infinite Love which works through Uni-

12. *Report of Addresses*, pp. 11–15.
13. *Report of Addresses*, pp. 16–29.

versal Law. 'Tis a good old word,—I like it. Gospel is "good news."
We have a new gospel of good news, a radical gospel, the gospel of
the "enthusiasm of humanity." God grant us power to publish this
gospel with the earnestness and self-sacrifice and fire of apostles,—
grant us a new Pentecostal outpouring of courage and fidelity to
truth! Now, as of old, the sneer will come,—"These men are drunk
with new wine!" And so we are. It *is* new wine, and is fast bursting
the old bottles. Friends, it is time to make new and better ones, fit
to receive the new vintage of God. Will you help us in the work of
today? [14]

Abbot in turn was repudiated by D. A. Wasson, the transcendentalist, who replied that any such humanistic theism would
be practically the same as atheism; for how could you conceive a
house from the mere properties of wood and clay? To the transcendentalist religion spoke in an absolute voice and with its own
logic. Wasson agreed that the old symbols of belief were broken,
but he denied Abbot's contention that the new faith must find its
validating experience solely in daily life or rational reflection.
Then as always, religion was the absolute affirmation of Spirit
welling up in the soul of man and carrying with it its own credentials.[15] The freedom of the new organization should have been
made clear by this time, although the reflective observer might
have wondered how durable it would prove when the time for positive action should come.

Colonel Higginson launched his share of the proceedings with
the chilling reminder that similar protests against denominationalism had been voiced by young radicals some twenty years
before, on almost the same spot of ground, and he confessed that
his ardor was somewhat dampened by the memory of the ephemeral character of those protests. He closed with the dreary observation that the spirit of the age was opposed to organization,
suggesting that the rebel had better stand alone with the general
sympathy of humanity behind him than rely on the feeble support
of a group. The session was closed by Emerson, who, in a few
sentences, went to the heart of the free religious idea. The church,
he observed, was no longer large enough for man. The old distinc-

14. *Report of Addresses*, pp. 37–40.
15. *Report of Addresses*, pp. 40–47.

tion between the church and the world would not do, for to modern man all aspects of life were equally sacred. If pure religion were to bear fruit in good works, however, it must organize itself, and he heartily endorsed the formation of the Free Religious Association.[16]

In the afternoon the Committee on Organization presented through Potter, its chairman, the draft of a Constitution virtually identical to that approved in the preliminary conference. Article I enumerated the objects of the Association: "to promote the interests of pure religion, to encourage the scientific study of theology, and to increase fellowship in the spirit." Any person in sympathy with these aims would be eligible for membership. Each member, however, according to Article II, would be responsible for his own opinions alone; nor should he consider his membership as affecting in any way his commitments to other organizations. Anyone wishing to enroll might do so without charge; but for the privilege of voting a membership fee of one dollar must be paid annually. Management of the affairs of the Association devolved upon an Executive Committee of thirteen, including the officers and six directors. Their duties, as defined by Articles III and IV, were to conduct the business of the Association in the interim between Annual Meetings, and to call special meetings or conventions to supplement the stated Annual Meeting to be held in Boston.[17] It will be observed that the Committee had no power to take any action or to determine policy for the Association.

The officers nominated by the Committee were elected at the afternoon session without discussion. Frothingham was chosen president. Robert Dale Owen, Thomas Wentworth Higginson, and Caroline M. Severance were vice-presidents. Potter and Rowland M. Conner, a radical Boston clergyman, were to be secretary and assistant secretary, respectively. Richard P. Hallowell, of a prominent Boston family, received the treasurership. The directors chosen included Rabbi Issac M. Wise, of Cincinnati; Charles K. Whipple, of Boston; Edward C. Towne; Frank B. Sanborn, of Concord; Hannah E. Stevenson, the friend of Parker and Whitman; and Ednah D. Cheney, the prominent women's rights leader.[18] At the conclusion of the meeting Secretary Potter en-

16. *Report of Addresses*, pp. 52–54.
17. *Report of Addresses*, pp. 54–55.
18. *Report of Addresses*, p. 55.

rolled the names of those wishing to join the Association. The first
to pay his dollar was **R. W. Emerson**.[19]

In many respects the organization meeting resembled the mem-
orable Chardon Street Convention of the "come-outers," in early
transcendentalist days, following in the same tradition of radical
revolt. Perhaps Colonel Higginson had that occasion in mind.
There was the same apparent lack of agreement obscuring an
intense earnestness lying beneath. The colonel did not give due
credit to "come-outerism" as the popular phase of transcendentalism, however, in charging it with voicing but a passing protest.
Higginson himself was ministering to a second generation of
"come-outers" in the Free Church of Worcester, for they formed
the backbone of his congregation of "Jerusalem wildcats." [20]
Samuel Johnson's Free Church of Lynn fell into the same category. In both cities, rapidly expanding with the new manu-
factures, but still dominated by the old Yankee laboring classes,
members of the middle and lower classes deserted the traditional
communions and flocked to hear the doctrines of spiritual freedom preached by these two transcendentalists. The fact that
both men were outspoken anti-slavery leaders helped to explain
the interest of common men and women in the sometimes nebulous
doctrines of transcendentalism, for the lower classes were generally more sympathetic to the anti-slavery crusade than were their
betters. Higginson noted the tendency of religious and social
radicalism to flourish especially in shoe towns like Lynn and
Abingdon. He concluded that "radicalism went with the smell of
leather." [21] Religious radicalism of a similar character grew rapidly throughout the Northeast and Midwest in the two decades
after the Civil War.[22] The Free Religious Association furnished
the germ of an organization and an intellectual leadership that
might have been capable of welding this sentiment into a liberal
movement of national importance had not the spirit of radical individualism nullified all efforts in this direction.

Statistical information concerning membership in the Association is extremely meager. At the Half-Century Anniversary of the
Association in 1917 a list of thirty-seven original members was

19. Potter, *The Free Religious Association*, p. 15 and note.
20. Higginson, *Cheerful Yesterdays*, pp. 130–131.
21. Higginson, *Cheerful Yesterdays*, pp. 114–115.
22. See Chapter VI.

published.[23] The names of Emerson and J. T. Sargent, aside from those of the officers, were the only ones which have survived in the memory of a later generation. The period of the Association's greatest activity was the mid-seventies, for which no membership statistics exist. In 1883 came the first statement of the number of members enrolled. Secretary F. A. Hinckley announced then that 250 members were distributed throughout eleven states and Canada, with about half of them concentrated in eastern Massachusetts.[24] Hinckley remarked that feeling in the Association was so sensitive on the subject of the freedom of its members that no notice was sent when membership expired. An unspecified number of persons, therefore, considered themselves members although their names did not appear on the rolls. Assuming that membership in the 'seventies reached the five hundred mark, the figure would still fall far below the 4,900-copy circulation figure of Abbot's *Index* in 1872, a year and a half after that magazine was founded.[25] Both institutions appealed to virtually the same people, and the failure of the Association to attract wider support reflected the desire of a majority of its members that it should confine itself to the dissemination of ideas.

Another reason why free religionists remained a numerically insignificant group was the difficulty of making clear what free religion was. Restatements of the meaning and aims of the Association at practically every Annual Meeting indicated the confusion of the religious world on the subject. At first glance the name "Free Religious Association" seemed to indicate that a common platform for all faiths was to be provided. This was true only in so far as the Association was concerned with the basic religious elements common to all religions. In no sense was it to be a battle ground for warring sects, or the mouthpiece of churches with dogmatic claims to the possession of the true dispensation. The Association, as Potter expressed it, extended a welcome to all religions, or to "so much of any religion as can prove itself to be true." [26] Here was revealed the rationalistic presupposition of the

23. From the program of the Half-Century Anniversary of the Free Religious Association, Boston, 1917.

24. F. R. A., Proceedings, 1883, *The Index*, n.s., III (June 7, 1883), 582–584.

25. See Chapter V.

26. F. R. A., *First Annual Report of the Executive Committee of the Free Religious Association, . . . 1868* (Boston, 1868), pp. 8–9. After 1868 the *Reports* were printed with the annual *Proceedings*.

group. Theological dogma must stand the test of scientific "proof" before it could be accepted by free religion. This positivistic attitude was somewhat in contradiction to the agnostic attitude of truth-seeking, which Potter declared almost in the same breath to be the cornerstone of free religion. The former position assumed that religious values were capable of "proof," and therefore were demonstrable. The latter assumed that each man must seek an individual solution to problems which were so highly personal that the authoritarian pronouncements of association or sect constituted an indefensible perversion of the truth. Frothingham confessed that the Association could not even prescribe what the standards of truth-seeking were.[27] One of the more disastrous divisions which rent the institutional life of the Association sprang from this philosophical contradiction. The scientific theists, following Abbot, clung to a theology which they would have promoted by every means in their power. The individualists, on the other hand, insisted so strongly upon the necessity of private judgment that positive institutional activity was out of the question. Orestes Brownson, then safe in the arms of Catholicism, touched upon the paradox when he remarked caustically that although free religionists believed individual reason and understanding to be relative and fallible, they insisted that all truth, knowledge, and reality as such were impersonal and absolute. If so, shrugged Brownson, how can such people be reasoned with? [28] These conflicting ideas naturally made exposition to the outside world difficult.

In drafting the constitution of the Association Abbot had been careful to define one of its objects to be the "scientific study of theology." There seems to be little doubt but that he intended it as an invitation to follow his own particular brand of scientific theism. Since science at that time carried connotations of freedom and truth for all religious liberals, the devotion of the Association to the scientific study of theology was taken for granted. The nebular hypothesis had replaced Creation according to Genesis,[29] and all theological dogmas must meet a similar test. In practice, however, the Association tended to stress only the broader aspect of science as the naturalistic study of the whole range of phenomema—historical, metaphysical, and natural, rather than the technically

27. F. R. A., *Proceedings, 1868*, pp. 20–21.
28. *The Catholic World*, X (Nov., 1869), 205.
29. F. R. A., *Proceedings, 1868*, pp. 22–23.

theological. Abbot's hopes for an official scientific free religion received another blow when Lucretia Mott successfully sponsored a constitutional amendment in 1874 altering the provision to read: "to encourage the scientific study of man's religious nature and history." The change reflected the opinion of many members that less emphasis should be put upon technical theological matters and more upon "pure religion" and social problems.[30]

Since the founders and organizers of the Association were all theists, and the constitution mentioned pure religion and the study of theology, agnostics and materialists outside the Association could scarcely be sure that they would receive a cordial welcome. Consequently, Abbot and Potter urged an amendment in 1872 making it clear that no form of theism was endorsed or prescribed for members. To Article II was added the provision that there should be "no test of speculative opinion or belief." [31] This amendment cleared the way for the entrance into the Association of Felix Adler and Benjamin Franklin Underwood, two of the most distinguished non-theists of the day.

With the appearance of non-theists in the front ranks of free religion after 1872 it was remarkable that a further contradiction in the Association's constitution should have remained undiscovered until 1885. In that year B. F. Underwood pointed to the inconsistency of an organization that claimed to be free, yet was dedicated by its constitution to the promotion of "the practical interests of pure religion." He argued that in the minds of the founders there had been a definite picture of what "pure religion" was, and that this picture had been sketched so many times in the colors of humanistic theism as to have given a special and restrictive meaning to pure religion. An ardent materialist, Underwood found the term unsatisfactory as a description of his own "spiritual" experience.[32] Although the expression "pure religion" might have been stretched to cover almost any kind of moral or emotional experience, and thus perhaps include Underwood's awareness of the laws of matter and energy, the force of his criticism was not lost upon the Association. The constitution was again amended to strike out the commitment to pure religion. The old Article I was divided into two articles:

30. F. R. A., *Proceedings, 1874*, pp. 5–6.
31. F. R. A., *Proceedings, 1872*, pp. 6–8.
32. F. R. A., Proceedings, 1885, *The Index*, n.s., V (June 4, 1885), 585.

Article I. This organization shall be called the Free Religious Association.

Article II. The objects of this Association are to encourage the scientific study of religion and ethics, to advocate freedom in religion, to increase fellowship in the spirit, and to emphasize the supremacy of practical morality in all the relations of life. All persons sympathizing with these aims are cordially invited to membership.[33]

These modifications in the constitution reflected the tendency of the Association to depart from the hopes of the founders that it would develop a rational and progressive religious faith. With the passing of the years emphasis was placed more upon the universal, non-sectarian aspect of free religion, and less upon its obligation to evolve and foster a religion specifically adapted to a rationalistic age. Francis Abbot placed the blame for this on the constitutional provision which prevented the Association from taking any action that might infringe the liberty of thought of any of its members. This self-denying ordinance virtually turned the Free Religious Association into a debating society.[34]

33. F. R. A., Proceedings, 1886, *The Index,* n.s., VI (June 3, 1886), 583.
34. See Chapter V.

## IV

## "THE FAITH OF REASON"—A RELIGION
## FOR DEMOCRACY

MAN'S desire for spiritual and intellectual unity in life is nowhere better seen than in his frequent attempts to impose logical relationships upon the most capricious of all subject matters, his own history. He seems to feel a deep-rooted esthetic distaste for the mutually contradictory ideas which often lie closely entwined in the life of any period, and he labors to explain away the discord with the aid of the historian's proverbial pack of tricks. The good Father Hecker, for instance, could not understand how democracy in America could evolve out of the determinism of misanthropic Calvinism. In order to free men's lives from that unnatural partnership he proposed a return to the freedom of Catholicism, where the true foundation of democracy, the Fatherhood of God and the brotherhood of man, was preserved inviolate. The equally earnest Francis Abbot trembled for the future of democracy in a nation which submitted to the slavish yoke of a spiritual kingdom where Christ was Lord and Master. Democracy could truly function, he believed, only when men recognized the supremacy of their own consciences, shaped by reason and knowledge, and oriented by a true conception of the Divine Power. Abbot explained away the fact that democracy had appeared before his views were widely held with the ingenious observation that the rise of democracy was the first triumph of free religion, not as yet consciously formulated. In accordance with the spirit of Abbot's criticism, the present chapter summarizes free religion as a faith prepared to spiritualize the secular, and to consecrate the common life. Unhampered by an authoritarian ideal or other-worldly considerations free religion offered itself as the authentic religion for democracy.

The Free Religious Association was no mere free platform where representatives of contending faiths might meet on equal footing. It was restricted to those who believed that the practical substance of "pure" religion was the ennoblement of man's life, regardless of their theoretical or "theological" grounds for so thinking.

Somewhat inconsistently, however, participation was at first limited further by the constitutional provision which betrayed the rationalistic presuppositions of the founders, namely, that the Association should dedicate itself to "the scientific study of theology." Anyone who accepted these restrictions might join, and erect on the base of universal religion any personal creed which pleased him. Free religion was the source, rather than the product, of the religious thinking of the Association. Contemporaries found it difficult to grasp this fact. Part of the misunderstanding was due to the absence of a clear statement of the exact character of the Association. Part was due to the stereotyped thinking prevalent in the orthodox churches. To most observers free religion meant anything the individual cared to believe; or better, no religion at all. Actually, free religion was a body of assumptions defining the life of the spirit in the nineteenth century, from which might grow a personal creed of theism, agnosticism, or materialism. Since these offshoots were to be recognized as faiths, not certainties like the free religion from which they sprang, they were to be held as tentative personal formulations, necessary to the individual who embraced them, but on no account to disrupt fellowship with those who accepted the certainties of free religion and then sought their explanation and origin along different paths.

It was natural that the destructive aspect of free religion should make a stronger impression upon the orthodox than its positive side. Moreover, the movement lacked a leader of the stature of Emerson or Parker about whom its affirmations might crystallize. It cannot be denied that the fundamental articles of free religion were difficult to grasp; and when formulated by so elusive a thinker as Frothingham his hearers were frequently left with little substance for their efforts to comprehend. Men with as little in common as Henry Ward Beecher and Henry Adams agreed in their dissatisfaction with free religion.[1]

In reviewing the principles that had governed his life work Frothingham agreed that he had assumed nothing as fixed in the spiritual life of man except "the validity of the human faculties, including, of course, the higher reason, the insight of genius, and such feelings as were parts of the rational constitution, together with perfect liberty in their exercise." The existence of God and

1. O. B. Frothingham, *The Weightier Matters of the Law: A Sermon* (New York, 1868), pp. 9–10. Henry Adams, *The Education of Henry Adams* (Boston and New York, 1918), p. 35.

the probability of immortality were discussed alike with evangelicals and materialists, and finally accepted as faiths insofar as
Deity seemed to be guaranteed by the fact of living mind, and immortality attested by individual persistency. Dogma and credo
were carefully avoided. "The object was to disintegrate, to pul-
-verize, to enable mind to float freely in the air of intellect, to the
end that it might crystallize about natural centers. All dogmatism,
that of the infidel as well as that of the believer, of the man of
science as well as of the theologian, of the sensualist as well as of
the spiritualist, was obnoxious." [2] Before articles of belief could be
formulated, the human mind must be emancipated from every
sort of thraldom, a task which would occupy men for some time to
come. This was the purely negative task Frothingham set for himself, and although his reticence surpassed that of many of his
fellows in the Free Religious Association who thought they had
defined the nature of things, he was by far the most famous radical,
and supplied most Americans with their picture of the free
religionist.

A statement of the free religious position must be made, then,
with the understanding that it represents the general sense of the
school, without implying that each idea was equally emphasized or
even acceptable to the thinking of all its members. Since Francis
Abbot, the most systematic thinker of the group, was in many
respects the least representative of free religion, it will not suffice
to summarize his own thought as the creed of his associates.

Basic to the thought of all was the conception of a religion, free
in the sense of being universal and rational. Christianity was
neither free nor rational, and the energy which free religionists
devoted to pointing out this fact proved eventually to be their
most effective work.

The age of rationalism which was culminating in the latter
nineteenth century with the perfection of the scientific method had,
according to free religion, so altered man's relation to his environment that religious problems, although still important, no longer
received adequate treatment at the hands of the clergy. For this
reason the most intelligent men of the modern world had repudiated
the traditional doctrines, and would continue to repudiate all
religious doctrines until religion could justify herself before the
bar of science.[3] It was an age of restatements. Every article of the

2. Frothingham, *Recollections,* pp. 139–141.
3. *Freedom and Fellowship in Religion,* pp. 1–5.

Christian faith was rejected by some competent scholar until there seemed to be no resource in the old creeds which could save the intelligent world from the slough of materialism. The free religionists were not so naive as to agree with many secularists that positive knowledge rendered religious faith unnecessary, but they did attribute the conflict between religion and science to the intransigent attitude of the Christian churches. Frothingham believed that the discouragement of the use of the intelligence practiced by all the churches left the individual little alternative but scepticism when he saw the creeds undermined by modern knowledge.[4]

Aside from its anti-intellectualism Christianity was attacked for its spiritual, moral, and ethical inadequacies. Needless to say, its cosmology and scriptural credentials were brushed aside with little attention, as having been effectively disposed of by a previous generation. Abbot, the most ardent anti-Christian of the group, gave the most effective formulation to this negative phase. The central core of Christianity was faith in Jesus as the "Christ of God," the Messiah. The fact that Unitarianism, the most liberal of the Christian churches, had recently pledged allegiance to Jesus as Lord and King was proof enough that the churches could not go beyond the confession and remain Christian. This was the only definition of Christianity which touched its unique essence, for its ethical and spiritual teachings were shared by many other faiths.[5] From the Christian Confession came the authoritarianism that had always distinguished the churches, culminating in Roman Catholicism. Protestantism, an inconsistent compromise between Catholicism and free religion, was, they said, doomed to extinction because of its contradictory character.[6]

The historical approach to the study of religions insisted upon by the free religionists was the fruit of the critical scholarship developed by the previous generation in Europe. If Jesus could have been shown to have been an original or creative figure, lifting the world to a higher spiritual level, focusing the religious forces of the day about His person, then Christianity might indeed claim to be a miraculous religion. But the messianic idea

4. Frothingham, *The Religion of Humanity* (New York, 1873), p. 30. *Creed and Conduct* (New York, 1877), pp. 28–32.

5. F. E. Abbot ("The Genius of Christianity and Free Religion"), *Freedom and Fellowship in Religion,* pp. 226–227.

6. F. R. A., *Proceedings, 1869,* p. 31–32. *Freedom and Fellowship in Religion,* pp. 232–233.

had been inherited from Judaism, and Jesus had led His age only
in transforming the prophesied material kingdom into a spiritual
one. As for the alleged spiritual supremacy of Jesus, who knew
the absolute depth of the religious consciousness of man? [7] Under
the impact of modern knowledge two new definitions of Christianity had attempted to salvage the Christian confession from the
corrosive acids of criticism. W. J. Potter termed them the liberal-
evangelical and the sentimental-historical definitions.[8] The
former, embraced by the liberal Protestant churches, although
it did not deny Jesus' messiahship, preferred to emphasize His
spiritual teachings: God's love for man, and man's love for God
and his fellow men. Its inspiration was found in the Scriptures.
This definition was declared to be defective in that it left uncertain the status of one who might practice the Christian virtues
while denying the Christian name. The latter definition, recently
developed in the writings of Seeley, Renan, Schenkel, and W. H.
Furness, emphasized the personal character of Jesus as the focal
point of a reverent, emotional religion. Christianity arose out of
enthusiasm for Jesus and His ideals. He was acknowledged the
earthly head of the Kingdom of God, the central figure of world
history, by virtue of His spiritual wisdom and historical significance. Potter proclaimed this definition also inadequate, for its
basis in the uniqueness of Jesus ignored the great historical forces
of the time which produced Him. Moreover, how could Jesus'
followers nineteen centuries afterwards be held by personal mag-
netism if not by the force of ideas? Potter himself proposed a
scientific-historical definition based on a scientific study of comparative religion. From such a definition, he was convinced, would
come the realization that the best elements of Christianity, the
ideas of the fatherhood of God and the brotherhood of man, were
not exclusively its own, but were universal.

The greatest defect of Christianity, however, was to be found
in its spiritual ideal. Abbot remarked, "There is but one ambition
sublimer than to *Reign by Serving*—and that is, to *Serve Without Reigning*. I cannot shut my eyes to the nobler purpose; I
cannot forget that Socrates both lived and died to make it real."
The Christian ideal was spiritual slavery, for there could be no

7. *Freedom and Fellowship in Religion*, pp. 238–245. F. R. A., *Proceedings,*
*1871*, p. 66.
8. W. J. Potter ("Christianity and Its Definitions"), *Freedom and Fellowship
in Religion*, pp. 190–201.

freedom except in reverence for the still, small voice within the soul as supreme over all other voices. If Christianity remained true to the ideals of its founder, it could not represent progressive life; it must remain a child's faith, supporting and guiding its communicants, instead of teaching them to rely upon their own self-respecting and self-controlling faith with the aid of conscious reason. As for the great spiritual and moral elements which made Christianity a religion, they were as widespread as man himself, and were to be found in one form or another in all faiths. Piety, purity, benevolence, mercy, forgiveness, self-sacrifice, love, prayer, repentance, faith, all were the substance of the divinest part of human nature, and appeared universally where man's highest aspirations were expressed.[9]

Not all of the radicals went so far as Abbot, Potter, and Frothingham in their denunciation of Christianity. In keeping the Unitarian name Weiss and Savage, for instance, were able to ignore the servitude implied in the Christian confession, while they found comfort and strength in its fellowship as long as they were allowed to rest in peace with their own definitions. That all were agreed Christianity must undergo at least far-reaching alterations, their membership in the Free Religious Association testified.

Abbot's *Impeachment of Christianity*[10] lacked the scurrilousness of Tom Paine's or Bob Ingersoll's denunciations of anthropomorphic religion, and it rested upon a different foundation from the old deistic ideas employed by those popular warriors. The idea, born from the study of comparative religion, that traditional Christianity, even though purged of its miraculous aspects, could not be identified with pure religion, was new in America. So also was the specific use by free religion of Emersonian spiritual self-reliance as an ideal against which the disciple of Christ might be displayed to his disadvantage. The free religious attack upon Christianity, save for its expression in *The Index*, was too intellectual to gain wide currency. But in liberal and especially Unitarian circles its influence was great, dissolving the old religious boundaries to such an extent that, by the twentieth century, Unitarianism was prepared to harbor theist and

9. *Freedom and Fellowship in Religion*, p. 249. F. R. A., *Proceedings, 1869*, pp. 36–37. *The Index*, I (January 8, 1870), 2–4.

10. F. E. Abbot, *The Impeachment of Christianity* (T. Scott's Publications. London, n.d.).

humanist indiscriminately. Nevertheless, there was considerably less agreement among free religionists in regard to the defects of Christianity than to the positive foundations of the faith of reason.

The fundamental assumption of free religion was the necessity of absolute freedom for the individual. Here was the prime consideration which had caused the break from Unitarianism. Not only did the radicals object to the Lordship of Jesus, but more than that they insisted that man should be bound by no creed. Ecclesiastical organization should prescribe nothing in respect to creed, and Abbot's substitute Preamble presented at Syracuse had embodied this idea. The insistence upon freedom was the great unifying thread running through all radical thought. Abbot found that as men, as thinkers, the delegates at Syracuse would have voted for freedom; but as Christians they could vote only for Christianity. Declaring that he loved freedom more than Christ, Abbot renounced Christianity.[11] That the revolt against Christian authoritarianism should occur in a democratic country was no coincidence. The Christian confession of the Lordship of Christ reflected the old monarchical ideal, which by the nineteenth century had given way to the democratic ideal. Freedom and democracy were synonymous terms, and Abbot considered free religion to be the highest spiritual development of democracy. As an authoritarian faith he suspected that Christianity was at heart unfriendly to free institutions. True Christianity, which he always held to be Catholicism, wished instinctively to dominate the political state, whereas free religion merely hoped to humanize it. A religion for democracy must assume that the human ideal in each of us "reflects the Divine Ideal above us as the dewdrop reflects the sun." [12]

Faith in democracy must be based upon a belief in the ability of men to regulate their affairs intelligently; and, similarly, faith in free religion, which placed the seat of religious authority within the soul of each man, required a belief in the essential rationality of men and things. In affirming such a conviction, the

11. J. F. Clarke and F. E. Abbot, *The Battle of Syracuse. Two Essays.* (The Index Tracts. no. 15. Boston, 1884). Reprinted from *The Index,* V (May 13 and 20, 1875), 18.

12. *The Index,* I (Jan. 22, 1870), 2–3; (Jan. 29), 2–3. F. E. Abbot, *Sectarianism, or Inclusiveness and Exclusiveness in Religion* (Free Church Tracts. no. 12. Tacoma, 1899), p. 3.

free religionists shared the characteristic rationalism of progressive thought in the later nineteenth century. The only method of analysis permissible in the examination of religious and physical phenomena alike was the scientific method. The Constitution of the Free Religious Association dedicated its members to the "scientific study of theology," and Abbot, who was responsible for this inclusion, called his own theology "Scientific Theism." [13] Chadwick entitled a characteristic volume of sermons *The Faith of Reason*, in which he held that all truths were to be discovered by observation, experiment, and reflection,[14] calling to mind Robert Ingersoll's "holy trinity" of reason, observation, and experience.

In its belief in the efficacy of scientific knowledge, as such, to promote human welfare, free religion shared the assumptions of the nineteenth-century science cult. At the close of his career, and in spite of some suggestions of a feeling of defeat, Frothingham penned an apostrophe to rationalism which compares in buoyancy with any paean ever sung by perfectionist:

The newest thing is knowledge. This never paralyzes, and never is fanatical. Its heart is stimulating yet gracious. Its zeal does not scorch or consume. It awakens every faculty, keeps inquiry on the stretch, excites the noblest ambition, and at the same time rebukes the partisan temper in all its manifestations. . . . For a long time to come there will be controversy, but its violence will disappear, its acrimony will gradually cease, the passion for victory will yield to the love of knowledge, and all genuine seekers will unite in the search after light.[15]

For the free religionist this faith in rationalism rested upon more than a mere awareness of the successes of the rationalistic method in the field of applied sciences. Unless he was willing to witness the suicide of the intelligence he felt compelled to postulate the unity of the universe; he must assume that law lay at the bottom of things, ultimately resolving apparently discordant and fortuitous events.[16] Here was another fundamental affirmation of free religion. The universal manifestation of law in nature gave

13. F. E. Abbot, *Scientific Theism* (Boston, 1885).
14. J. W. Chadwick, *The Faith of Reason* (Boston, 1879), pp. 81–84.
15. Frothingham, *Recollections,* p. 143.
16. Abbot, in *The Christian Examiner,* 5 ser., XVII (Sept., 1865), 164.

all the evidence necessary to believe in God, Providence, and spiritual values. As Chadwick expressed it, "The more law, the more God." [17] Abbot preferred to see in the uniformities of nature evidence of a conscious and rational Personality.[18] Chadwick, following Herbert Spencer, saw the old multiplicity of mysteries which had peopled the world with gods in ancient times giving way to one great mystery, the principle of uniformity, which still elicited man's awe and adoration. In either case the premise was the same. Frothingham stated categorically that "the Radical believes in universal law, omnipotent, omnipresent, sweeping through the world, administering the least things, controlling the greatest, holding close relations between you and me, holding in the hollow of its hand all the affairs of all the nations of the globe. This idea of law—material, intellectual, spiritual—comprehends everything." [19]

In addition to discovering the uniformity of the natural order, rationalism, or the scientific method, produced most fruitful results when applied to the study of man's religious history. Following the interest of Emerson in the Oriental religions, and relying heavily upon the studies of Max Mueller, the radicals pioneered in the introduction of the study of comparative religion in America. Their interest was scarcely scientific in the best sense. They frankly sought the universal agreements which would confirm their theory that beneath all historical faiths lay that pure and universal religion which was the natural if unconscious result of man's experience in a world of eternal law. Beneath the diversity of religious practices could be found the great universal religious ideas: God, Duty, Benevolence, and Immortality. Polytheism when examined, for instance, generally revealed the belief in a supreme creator underlying its multiplicity of deities. Potter believed that the universality of these ideas indicated that they were native to the human consciousness. Even though one might have speculative difficulties about God or immortality he could recognize the historical force of those ideas and participate in a religious fellowship in which righteousness would consecrate his

17. Chadwick, *The Faith of Reason*, p. 95.
18. Abbot stated his theology in semi-popular form in *The Way Out of Agnosticism, or the Philosophy of Free Religion* (2nd ed., Boston, 1890). His system finally stated in full philosophical dress appeared in *The Syllogistic Philosophy, or Prolegomena to Science* (2 vols., Boston, 1906).
19. *The North American Review*, CXL (April, 1885), 321.

life. Free religionists believed that realization of these facts laid the basis of a truly world-wide "Broad Church." As men came to feel their natural spiritual unity they would begin to yearn for a universal faith which would lift them above the differences of creed into a common fellowship. In free religion the radicals proposed to offer such a faith.[20]

Evolution, the latest product of rationalistic thought, was entirely acceptable to the new religious thinking. The older radicals were evolutionists before Darwin. Such younger men as Abbot, Potter, and Chadwick, found the evolutionary theory at the very basis of their faith. Frothingham declared that thereafter all religious thought must start with the fact of evolution as its strongest credential;[21] while Minot Savage claimed to be the first man in America to preach a gospel of evolution literally inspired by the Darwinian and Spencerian systems.[22] The course of evolution displayed the workings of Deity, as higher forms were developed out of lower. When the stage of civilization was reached the evolutionary view assumed that society should be seen as an organically developing creature. Here the moral element entered the evolutionary process, fundamentally altering the method by which it worked, and indicating the power of self-development by which the race was now its own reformer and savior. The implication of all this for the old religious thinking was self-evident. Formerly God had been considered responsible for human progress. The spiritual interpretation of evolution now showed that man was responsible for his own development.[23]

The end of evolution or progress was the perfect society. Free religionists admitted it unblushingly, for it was no absurdity to be a social perfectionist in the nineteenth century. Abbot declared the whole aim of free religion to be "the symmetrical development of Human Nature in all directions, the Perfection of the Individual and the Perfection of the Race." [24] In view of the free religious belief that Deity was working through the natural processes it was not surprising that D. A. Wasson should define the

20. F. R. A., *Proceedings, 1871*, p. 51. Samuel Longfellow ("The Unity and Universality of Religious Ideas"), in *Freedom and Fellowship in Religion*, pp. 46–49, 58. *The Index,* I (Jan. 15, 1870), 2–3.
21. Frothingham, *Creed and Conduct,* p. 12.
22. *The Christian Register,* LXII, no. 13 (Mar. 29, 1883), 194.
23. Frothingham, *The Religion of Humanity,* pp. 169–170.
24. *The Index,* I (Jan. 15, 1870), 2–3.

essence of human nature as the dream of perfection. All of man's distinctive genius was in it, and all of his highest performance came out of it. "It hovers before him as an ideal, and makes the impulse, the guidance, and the goal of progress." The later nineteenth century might be an age of agnosticism, the "drift period," as Frothingham called it, taking his terminology from geology, as the deists before him had drawn theirs from mechanics, but it was only a spiritual interregnum, in which a vast plan of democratic human comforts was being realized. Eventually, as Emerson had said, "a new Socrates, or Zeno, or Swedenborg, or Pascal, or a new crop of geniuses, . . . with happy heat and a bias for theism," would inaugurate the new age of spiritual values, in which man would be recognized to be the outgrowth of divine life.[25]

The goal of mundane perfection was the free religious counterpart of the Heavenly goal of traditional religion. Faith in man's capacity for self-improvement was based upon the potentialities of human nature rather than upon present reality, and the chief means of realizing these potentialities would be universal compulsory education.[26] To set up the goal of a fully developed life as a religious ideal tended to destroy the distinction between the religious and the secular. Every aspect of life became religious. Every act was an act of worship, while the older formalized worship as practiced by the creeds sank to a position of insignificance. As Frothingham expressed it, once the character of the faith consistent with modern knowledge has been determined, "the next step in the development of free thought must be toward the realization of all the ideal supports of mankind, the spiritualizing of the secular, the lifting into heavenly places of this world's activity, the transfiguration of our common life. . . . That there is no final truth discoverable must be admitted, but such a confession need not trouble those who look manfully forward to a future of new discoveries, and gird themselves to remove all obstacles to the knowledge of the world they live in." [27] Frothingham's scepticism was not shared by the other radicals, but his humanism was common to them all. If free religion was man's effort to perfect himself, it must be concerned with the affairs of everyday life.

25. *Freedom and Fellowship in Religion,* pp. 370–372. Emerson, *Journals,* X (1864), 9. Wasson, *Essays,* p. 108.
26. Abbot, *Compulsory Education* (Index Tracts. no. 7. Toledo, 1871), p. 2.
27. Frothingham, *Recollections,* p. 44.

No one denied the implication, although considerable difference of opinion existed among its members as to whether the Free Religious Association should itself take the lead in the work of social reform, or should confine itself to the propagation of the new ideas, leaving their practical application to other agencies. Felix Adler broke with the Association because the latter view prevailed. This was, however, merely a matter of the most advisable division of labor, for nearly all of those connected with the movement were ardent humanitarians.

In its practical application, free religion appeared to be a form of religious humanism, although it was far from being a mere preview of twentieth-century humanism. Contemporaries might understandably brand the radicals as godless infidels if they were to lift out of their context random statements such as the following from a Frothingham sermon: "Suffuse social science with the warm, glowing sentiments of reverence, aspiration, devotion, and you will make it a noble religion." [28] Yet, if the critic were to turn to the same writer's *Religion of Humanity*, the title of which was borrowed from Auguste Comte's positivist religion, he would nevertheless find there a criticism of Comte, precisely because Comte made mankind the only God man can know. Frothingham insisted that humanity in the highest sense is but a reflection of Deity. The destruction of the human species could not involve the destruction of the first cause of the universe.[29] Although the delicate balance between humanism and theism was not maintained by all the members of the Association, it was the characteristic position of the group.

The definitions of religion most satisfactory to the radicals were formulated by Abbot. "Religion is not mere thinking or mere feeling or mere doing, not mere belief or mere sentiment or mere action, but LIVING UPWARD, which is all of them in one"; it is striving to achieve knowledge, love, and virtue. It is "man's obedience to that something within him which ever impels him upward to the Better." "It is the soul's deep resolve to love the truth, to learn the truth, and to live the truth, uncoerced and free." It affirms the right to think; the rights of conscience; that a higher law exists; and that universal law and transcendent love are identical. This was "pure" religion, the absolute religion of

28. Frothingham, *The Weightier Matters of the Law* (New York, 1868), p. 21.
29. Frothingham, *The Religion of Humanity*, pp. 105–107.

Parker freed from the primitive Christianity with which he had identified it.[30]

There was nothing arbitrary about these definitions. They described the universal essence of all religions. The scientific spirit of inquiry applied to the world's faiths revealed as the central idea of each a theory of man's relation to the universe and its vital forces. It also revealed an invariable sense of obligation to maintain the proper relationship to these powers. Ideas as to the nature of this law of obligation might vary widely, from a low conception of it as the arbitrary will of gods and demons to the highest conviction of the necessary moral relations inherent in the very nature of things, independent of all will, and appealing to love of virtue for its own sake. This universal tendency of man to seek a proper orientation to the cosmos did not spring from the mandate of special revelation, as nearly all of the historical faiths insisted, nor from a super-rational intuition implanted in the soul of each man, as the transcendentalists would have affirmed. It appeared rather through a process that might be called "social Lamarckism." The religious feeling had been wrought into man by the cosmic and social forces in which he had lived from immemorial times, until what had been gradually acquired by experience became intuition. Thus faith in God was held to be the flower of hereditary experience.[31]

From attributing the cause of all religious emotion to the sense of relationship to the universe certain conclusions about the nature of the universe followed inevitably. Wasson held that it must be an all-inclusive system, since if there were anything outside it would be no universe. Likewise, it must be unified, since a discordant universe would destroy itself. All would concede that it produces man and his mind; and since it could hardly produce its superior, even if the presence of man's mind in a materialistic, uncomprehending world were intelligible, the rational theists and transcendentalists agreed that the universe was, therefore, a luminous spiritual whole, open and akin to the mind of man.[32]

30. Abbot, *Sectarianism*, p. 3. *The Index*, I (Jan. 15, 1870), 2. *Freedom and Fellowship in Religion*, p. 253.

31. *The Index*, n.s., II (Jan. 5, 1882), 317–318. Abbot, *Free Religion in a Free State. Gleanings from Francis E. Abbot's Writings. Selected, prepared, and published by Ross Winans* (Baltimore, 1872), pp. 3–4. Chadwick, *The Faith of Reason*, pp. 81–84.

32. D. A. Wasson ("The Nature of Religion"), in *Freedom and Fellowship in Religion*, pp. 25–31.

Thus the religious tendency was seen to be a prophetic impulse guiding man to the center of all Being. The problem of freedom, which was such a stumbling block for many religions, was solved, in the opinion of Johnson and Frothingham, through a proper understanding of the law of evolution. By definition, progress, or evolution, could have as its goal nothing less than the realization of the Infinite, and in recognizing that infinity was implicated in his own finite conditions man achieved freedom.[33]

Having established religion as the problem of man's relation to the universe the free religionists failed to agree in their analysis of the character of the vital powers of that universe. Those who were theists varied considerably in the qualities with which they endowed their Deity. The agnostics conceded the probability of vital powers but refused to speculate as to their nature. The materialists spoke of matter and energy as the ultimate realities, and sought a purely utilitarian basis for ethics. The common platform of free religion on which all were united in the Association proved to be an inadequate basis for fellowship, given such divergent opinions. Within fifteen years internal stresses began to appear which shortly put an end to the useful career of the Association.[34] Friction developed over both the relation of free religion to Christianity and the meaning of free religion itself as the practical embodiment of efforts to advance social welfare. These differences derived in the last analysis from the various views of the fundamental religious problems entertained by the members of the Association. It is safe to conclude, therefore, that the common foundation which was assumed to underlie all valid religious experience was unable to furnish a bond strong enough to hold together those who accepted the premise.

Among the theists, Abbot's conception of Deity was the most compelling because it was the most personal. In all true religious worship, he believed, the object of adoration must be an objective Person. It could be no pantheistic personality first attaining self-consciousness in the breast of the worshipper, but must be possessed of the same order of personality as all human beings. From the individual to this Personality, the eternal Infinite, the hier-

33. Abbot, "Theism and Christianity," *The Christian Examiner,* 5 ser., XVII (Sept., 1865), 164–165. *Freedom and Fellowship in Religion,* pp. 94–96; *The Christian Examiner,* 5 ser., XVII (July, 1865), 21–23.
34. See Chapters V and VII.

archy of existence was conceived to be a system of concentric circles, the outer including the inner. "Narrow as is the human, it is yet concentric with the divine. Whatever transcendent attributes belong to God, and with insufferable radiance shield from profane inspection the eternal mystery of the I AM, still Religion must believe them compatible with the wisdom, power, and goodness, without which he is no God to her. The human, to the poor extent of its tether, coincides with the divine." Religion, therefore, presupposes "the Finite Divinity of man, and the Infinite Humanity of God." [35] Conceived in such terms, Abbot's personal faith possessed a vividness and emotional fervor denied to the creeds of many of his associates.

Frothingham, less of a logician than Abbot, conceived of God not as a person but as a Force in nature, a Principle or Influence; a vague, indefinite, unconscious Power pervading the universe. Such a Deity could not be prayed to or worshipped in religious exercises. He was to be thought of as the Ideal Being, comprehending all the qualities of personality, but to be communed with only by living to the best of one's ability. Piety consisted in living for some good and worthy end: from philanthropy and reform to the humblest daily tasks honestly performed.[36]

Also numbered among the theists were the younger transcendentalists and the "Cosmists," as the followers of Herbert Spencer called themselves. An important distinction which separated them in their thinking indicated the difference of their mental temper. The transcendentalists, of whom Samuel Johnson was representative, clung to the Emersonian concept of the Over-Soul, the transcendent universal Mind. Following the lead of the Concord seer, Johnson maintained that the evolution of higher forms out of lower in the natural sphere could only be explained on the assumption that the process was a "drawing out" of Mind.[37] The Cosmists, on the other hand, conceived of Deity as purely immanent, and inseparable from the material universe of which it was the soul. Many of the attributes of Deity must remain unknown to men. Certainly personality, which would be a limitation, was not one of them. As much as men knew of the universe so

35. Abbot, in *The Christian Examiner,* 5 ser., XVII (Sept., 1865), 165–166.
36. Frothingham, *Vital Piety. A Sermon.* (New York, 1872), p. 13. Cf. Frothingham, *Creed and Deed,* pp. 12–14.
37. *Freedom and Fellowship in Religion,* p. 95.

much they knew of God. Thus theology became the science of sciences.[38] "If this be pantheism," cried Chadwick, "make the most of it!" Pantheism in one form or another, he insisted, had always been the creed of the most enlightened souls. Frothingham likewise saw the religious thought of the day tending toward a vague pantheism. Unlike theism, which he believed to be too cold and intellectual for wide appeal, pantheism excited the imagination, used the symbolism of nature, and even restored the majesty of the traditional creeds previously destroyed by rationalism. It also reconciled the old religious problem of free will and determinism, for to be free under the laws of nature was to be bound, and to be bound by the laws of the spirit was to be free.[39] The transcendentalists, however, declared the utilitarian tendencies of the Cosmists to be the highroad to materialism, and with the passing of the years the sympathy between these two groups of theists gradually wore thin.[40]

There was nothing in the free religious platform which denied the status of a "religion" to atheism in its various forms, although no professed atheists joined the Association. As long as an individual felt and responded to an inward ethical imperative he was a religious person, whether he ascribed the source to be God, impersonal force, or the laws of matter. Chadwick believed that the agnostic might deny a theory of the universe which presupposed God, but as long as he came to grips with the cosmic order of things he had the essence of religion. In short, morality became religious when it became voluntary devotion to the eternal order of the universe.[41] Felix Adler, the leading agnostic, cordially accepted the free religious position as a basis for coöperation. Upon it he built his own religion of agnosticism. Due to man's finite understanding there was no possibility of comprehending the infinite with certainty, therefore Adler could hold none of the traditional or modern theistic assumptions as fundamental to religion. The individual felt the moral texture of things in himself and in the universe, religion consisting in the ordering of one's

38. Savage, *Belief in God,* pp. 27–28, 35–39.

39. Chadwick, *The Faith of Reason,* pp. 97–103, 113. Frothingham, in *The Christian Examiner,* 5 ser., XVII (July, 1865), 19–23.

40. Johnson, *Lectures,* pp. 127, 129.

41. *The Index,* I (Jan. 15, 1870), 2. Chadwick, *The Faith of Reason,* pp. 36–40, 65.

life accordingly. It was true that people had customarily assigned this tendency toward the good to the influence of an omnipotent, omniscient, all-loving God, but such an idea Adler declared to be drawn from finite experience, having no meaning when applied to the infinite. Thus when asked what was the source of his confidence in the good purpose of the universe he would reply that he did not know. It was enough for him to know that life here has meaning, that it tends toward moral perfection, and that in spite of its sorrows and afflictions it is bound to culminate in a sublime dénouement. In moments of doubt, Adler, who had lost his faith in the power of prayer as used for such purposes by the orthodox, was accustomed to practice good deeds, thus regaining his belief in them. His insistence upon action as the best antidote for scepticism proved to be the blade which severed his allegiance to the Association.[42] As it became more clear that the Association would confine itself merely to discussion of the religious problem, Adler's dissatisfaction increased. He resigned in 1882 the presidency he had held since 1879, and devoted his efforts exclusively to the practical social work of his Society for Ethical Culture in New York.

Forced to abandon theism as a basis for practical coöperation, free religion likewise took no position on the question of personal immortality. The variety of views on the subject entertained by members of the Association indicated the difficulties which the problem presented for rationalistic thought. The transcendentalists quite generally clung to immortality on the basis of its universal appearance in world religions. Chadwick, the chief sources of whose thought were utilitarianism and Spencer, retained his belief in spiritual survival on no stronger ground than that of an instinctive faith.[43] Weiss solved the problem by asserting that there was no such thing as death. "There is nothing really inanimate in all creation; for the Infinite Life has gone into representation by each. of its epochs, from the primordial germinal matter through all its evolutions: no form or result of it can be dead. There is no such thing as death, but an incessant shifting into and out of all forms." Frothingham and Abbot, on the other hand, rejected the hope of immortality since it could not be sub-

42. F. R. A., *Proceedings, 1882,* pp. 606–607.
43. Chadwick, *The Faith of Reason,* p. 126.

stantiated by rational thought. If a higher life is to follow this one, said Abbot, that will be time enough for it. But "before heaven above, heaven below." [44]

A religion with humanistic orientation must inevitably have considerable to say concerning problems of ethics. In this field free religion introduced to America important new tendencies in European thought which were to take root and blossom in many phases of American thinking in the twentieth century. Evolution was the great single source of the new thinking. The modern moralist was confronted with entirely new conditions to which his thinking must be aligned. Neither the universe nor society could any longer be conceived of as static organizations, but must be considered to be in a constant process of change. Since the rational theist rejected the Christian assumption that morality had been imposed upon nature by an arbitrary Deity, arguing for a rational morality inhering in the nature of things, he must now introduce flexibility into ethical standards while preserving human conduct from purely selfish expediency. The transcendentalists had been the last of the liberal thinkers privileged to retain an absolute standard of ethics. Following the evolutionary impulse the post-Darwinian thinker could not conceal from himself the fact that moral standards changed from age to age. The ethical import of an act was determined by the conditions and beliefs of the day in which it was committed.[45]

Chadwick declared the greatest good of the greatest number at any moment to be the end of all morality. Frothingham reluctantly agreed to the extent that "the experience of humanity begets the conscience of humanity." The radicals were quick to defend their universal hedonism against the charge of selfishness. Each man had the right and duty to strive for the highest possible good, and the protection of his right became the duty of all. The utilitarian morality was based upon the supposition of a vast and little-understood order of development, representing the growing consciousness of that fact in the minds of men. The fact of men living together in society had gradually developed conscience.

44. *Freedom and Fellowship in Religion,* pp. 159–161. Frothingham, *The Religion of Humanity,* pp. 233–264. *The Index,* I (Jan. 15, 1870), 3. F. R. A., *Proceedings, 1870,* p. 45.

45. F. R. A., *Proceedings, 1879,* pp. 22–24. Frothingham, *The Religion of Humanity,* p. 284.

For out of primitive struggle had come the realization that men must adjust their desires to the needs of others. This realization Chadwick termed variously the Moral Law, the Law of Liberty, or Conscience. "Right" was the science necessary to the art of living together, and each owed its practice to all.[46] The new hedonism proposed to maintain a balance between the egoism of the Golden Rule, in which personal desires determined ethical values, and the submergence of the individual in the general welfare, advocated by Comtean positivism. Neither egoism nor altruism was the ideal, but "relativism." As opposed to the Christian emphasis upon devoutness, humility, submission, reverence for authority, and reliance upon the personal conscience, the new ethics would stress intelligence, manliness, moral earnestness, humanity, enthusiasm for natural justice, and the ardor of natural kindness. These new values were the answer of the free religionists to the charge frequently heard, that their movement owed its strength and ideas to the humanistic tradition which had always flourished within the Christian church.[47]

The new ethics were to stem from the fact that the one changeless factor in a world of change was the existence of society, with the obligation to maintain it. To assure the continuance and improvement of society was the purpose of social science, one aspect of which, dealing with problems involving the activities of the individual, might be called "moral science."[48] For society as a whole, the aim of free religion was to secure the perfection of mankind. Although the Free Religious Association decided that the actual work of reform should be left to other agencies, the intellectual and spiritual stimulation should find its source in organized free religion.

The new ethical relativism was consistent with the empirical approach of free religion to the materials of universal religious and social experience. It foreshadowed important trends in twentieth-century thought. Not all of the free religionists, however, were prepared to accept experimentalism in ethics. The transcendentalists, who were also the older members of the group, found the moral law as well as the religious sentiments graven in

46. F. R. A., *Proceedings, 1879*, pp. 24–32.
47. Frothingham, *The Religion of Humanity*, pp. 177–179. *Creed and Conduct*, pp. 18–19.
48. *The Christian Examiner*, 5 ser., XVII (July, 1865), 25.

the soul, and their conservatism influenced them in interpreting the moral law in a traditional fashion.[49] Although Abbot's scientific theists accepted the evolutionary development of ethical ideas and insisted that a truly scientific or rationalistic approach to ethics would yield a morality nobler perhaps than any that yet prevailed, they nevertheless shrank from the full consequences of ethical relativism. Abbot maintained that ethical systems were slow to change, and that each system must be compulsive within the society and epoch embracing it. Only as the highest and most refined experience of the race justified it could prevailing moral precepts be altered to conform to new social and religious ideals. In practice, Abbot led the attack upon his fellow radicals who urged hasty modification of the Victorian morality of the Gilded Age.[50] The inability of free religion to agree upon a new ethical orientation was a further factor tending to undermine its solidarity with the passage of the years.

The society of tomorrow, in which free religion would be realized, was delineated in glowing terms by Abbot. Individuals and society would undergo a constant process of improvement by means of education and scientific rehabilitation. The state becomes a voluntary association of individuals dedicated to one another's welfare. A Congress of Nations coördinates the states and transacts the world's governmental business. "Competition will become rivalry in coöperation." Racial and national distinctions are submerged in the growing consciousness of the common nature and destiny of mankind. Church and state are identical, although strictly speaking the state absorbs all religious functions. As an organization, free religion would probably hold weekly services for worship and mutual improvement, at which all subjects concerning human welfare would be discussed. Free Societies would also devote themselves to practical philanthropy and social reform. Membership would be conditioned merely upon willingness to coöperate in benefiting mankind; and Christian, Jew, and Atheist would be welcome.[51] Such was the mundane ideal that sustained free religion.

49. *The Index*, III (Feb. 10, 1872), 41–44.
50. See pp. 118–129.
51. *The Index*, I (Feb. 5, 1870), 2–3.

# V

## "A VOICE WITHOUT A HAND"

THE Free Religious Association was conceived by the extreme radicals as a substitute for the organizations of Unitarianism. In a real sense it was a sort of mutual protective society for those dissenters who would not submit to the yoke of Christ, as prescribed by the National Unitarian Conference. The prime movers of the new organization were Abbot and Potter, the most outspoken critics of the denomination. From a study of the existing records it is difficult to avoid the feeling that to a considerable extent the formation of the Association was prompted by purely negative considerations; men needed a new fellowship to replace the old one no longer available. On the other hand, the radicals had a natural desire to establish a platform for the dissemination of their ideas, and in that sense the Association had a unique function. Since the essence of free religion, however, lay in its universal, non-sectarian character it was difficult to devise a program which would satisfy the wide variety of dissidents who sought refuge beneath the new banner, each with his own particular grievance and nostrum. To this must be added the fact that many members and friends never fully grasped the meaning of free religion or sensed its true relation to orthodox religious thought of all types. These circumstances raised difficulties which the Association never overcame, and they eventually destroyed its usefulness.

According to its Constitution, the objects of the Association were to "promote the interests of pure religion, to encourage the scientific study of theology, and to increase fellowship in the spirit." [1] Into these general phrases may be read the entire meaning of free religion, but read more easily by the historian with the benefit of hindsight and careful study than by the contemporary who might wish to know what specific activity the new Association would pursue. The elucidation of the general principles of the

1. *Report of Addresses at a Meeting Held in Boston, May 30, 1867, to Consider the Conditions, Wants, and Prospects of Free Religion in America* (Boston, 1867), pp. 54–55.

Constitution was left to the Executive Committee, composed of the officers and directors.[2] The committee met some ten times before the first Annual Meeting in May, 1868, although it had no headquarters or regular place of meeting. No policy or program of action was formulated. Secretary Potter, in his first annual report, expressed no surprise or disappointment at this, for he assumed that it was generally understood that the progressive religious spirit must work out its own results independently of organized action. The aim of the Association was to strengthen the groups spontaneously attracted to it by providing a common platform on which each member might rear his own system of thought.[3] Years later, however, Potter recalled that he had soon realized that the constitutional provision that had left members of the Association responsible for their own opinions alone and had imposed no restrictions upon their relations with other organizations (Article II) admitted such a wide variety of thought to the Association that positive action became virtually impossible.[4] Since the officers and directors had been carefully selected to represent this diversity, it was not surprising that the committee meetings should early make the problem evident.

All were agreed, however, that the basic principles of free religion should be spread through tracts and lectures, if not by more aggressive missionary methods, and for this purpose funds were needed. Receipts from membership fees and private donations for the first year amounted to $741.45, of which $505.96 was appropriated to meet the expenses of the first meeting, print its proceedings, and conduct correspondence. In reporting these figures at the second meeting, R. P. Hallowell, the treasurer, remarked that his appeals for donations would meet with more success if he could present a specific program of action on which the money would be spent. For himself, he believed that the Association should devote itself to the promotion of pure religion and wider fellowship, forgetting scientific theology. The latter interest would absorb the energies of radicals to the exclusion of practical religious concerns, as well as destroy harmony. He insisted that preoccupation with theological problems intellectualized religious conceptions and thereby sapped their vitality. He quoted a sentence from the *Radical* as a case in point. "The fatal error of

2. Potter, *The Free Religious Association*, p. 16.
3. F. R. A., *First Annual Report of the Executive Committee of the Free Religious Association . . . May 28, 1868* (Boston, 1868), pp. 3–5.
4. Potter, *The Free Religious Association*, pp. 16–17.

Calvin's theory," it read, "consisted in simply forgetting that the equation must be freed from the anthropocentric parallax." Hallowell defied anyone to expound the meaning of this riddle. "Friends," he cried, "it is time to lay aside such drivel. . . . Divorce religion from theology if you wish to become in truth a *free* religious association." [5] Hallowell's blast opened the struggle between the intellectual and practical wings in the Association which continued for the next twenty-five years.

Free religion was frequently defined as the universal religious sentiment running through all special religions. Belief in God, immortality, moral obligation, and the integrity of the personality were elements of it found in some measure wherever men existed. Several early meetings of the Association were employed to dramatize the idea by inviting leading representatives of Christian and non-Christian sects to share the platform, each discussing his own faith in the light of its basic principles in order to bring out underlying agreements. The device, which was first used in 1868 and again in 1870, was not, on the surface at least, too successful. On the former occasion a Unitarian, a Baptist, an Episcopalian, and a Universalist each spoke for his own creed, although the committee had carefully selected liberals from each denomination. The Catholic priest who had been invited refused to attend. James Freeman Clarke, representing Unitarianism, insisted that Christianity was as broad as religion itself. Modern conceptions of freedom, progress, and humanity were all based upon it. Clarke implied that without the careful preparation of Christianity the Free Religious Association would scarcely be able to exist. Needless to say, he made no mention of the Lordship of Jesus or the Christian confession. The testimony of the other Protestants was as unsatisfactory from the radical point of view. Charles H. Malcom, the Baptist, insisted upon the right of individual interpretation of the Bible. This was no more than a reaffirmation of the traditional Protestant position. Free religionists well knew its divisive and sectarian influence upon American religion. A religion not based upon Scripture was apparently inconceivable to Malcom. The Universalist, Olympia Brown, took a similarly orthodox position. [6] The hope of the free religionists that a picture of absolute religion would emerge did not materialize from this symposium.

5. F. R. A., *Proceedings, 1868*, pp. 17–18.
6. F. R. A., *Proceedings, 1868*, pp. 24–52.

On returning to the theme in 1870 the committee kept matters in its own hands. The field was extended to cover all of the world's great religions, but the labor of exposition was entrusted to friends. Samuel Johnson, who kept aloof from the Association for conscientious reasons, but who was sympathetic to its purposes, read a paper on "The Natural Sympathy of Religions." [7] He believed that it was time "for our scholarship to demonstrate the unity of the religious sentiment, and the ethical brotherhood of the race, from a point of view broad enough at once to rebuke the contempt of weaker races by the strong, to silence the pretenses of religious monopoly, and to break the dream of exclusive revelation, so thoroughly that no sane or even honest faith shall ever be heard again proclaiming that all who came before itself were thieves and robbers in the fold of God." Rabbi Wise spoke for Judaism, which he conceived to be the oldest Free Religious Association. Its God had been universalized since the days of Moses, and it recognized no Messiah but Truth and Reason. [8] This was the sort of thing the radicals wanted to hear. The resourceful Colonel Higginson spoke on Mohammedanism; William Henry Channing, on the religions of China; and Potter, on the religions of India. [9] The religious situation in the latter country was especially interesting to the radicals. The interaction of many faiths in India was found to have produced in the Brahmo-Somaj a form of pure theism similar to that professed by a majority of the free religionists. In stressing the similarity of spiritual ideals among the great religions the radicals were making one of their most important contributions to American religious thinking.

Another type of activity favorably regarded by all elements in the Association was the spread of free religious ideas by means of the lecture platform. No sooner had free religion been organized than a vigorous attempt was made to carry the fight into the enemy camp. A series of lectures to be held in Cambridge for the purpose of reaching the Harvard Divinity School students was planned by the committee. When action was jeopardized by the failure of the committee to raise a quorum at its October, 1867, meeting, Potter arranged the lectures by securing private donations. They were given during the academic year 1867–1868 by leaders of the Association, and emphasized progressive and ra-

---

7. F. R. A., *Proceedings, 1870*, pp. 59–81.
8. F. R. A., *Proceedings, 1870*, pp. 84–89.
9. F. R. A., *Proceedings, 1870*, pp. 90–119.

tionalistic religious ideas.[10] No detailed report of these lectures has been found, but their effect on the Divinity School students was attested by C. W. Wendte, then a student at the school, and later President of the Free Religious Association (1910–1914). Wendte recalled that the students were so captivated by the new ideas that the class of 1868 invited John Weiss to be their class preacher, the class of 1869 extending a similar invitation to Frothingham. The Society for Promoting Theological Education, a conservative Unitarian group then constituting the board of overseers of the school, was greatly disturbed, and set up a committee to look into affairs. The members of the class of 1869 were examined individually as to their personal views on the Christian religion. As a result of the inquisition two men were refused the annual stipend, or scholarship, usually granted to all students; and the remainder of the class, save one, promptly refused theirs. After some delay the matter was cleared up to the professed satisfaction of all concerned, although the real victory was won by the students. A similar attempt at personal catechism undertaken at Meadville Theological Seminary, the other Unitarian stronghold, also failed.[11]

Heartened by the success of the Cambridge lectures, since the disturbance created was out of all proportion to the numbers attending, Potter organized the Horticultural Hall Lectures, to be given in that well-known auditorium in Boston the following winter. The aim again was to spread free religious ideas, although in a more popular form in order to attract general interest. A similar series of lectures was given there annually until 1878, the Executive Committee of the Association taking charge of them after 1871.[12] The subjects of the lectures, each delivered by a leading radical, were at first closely restricted to the problems of rational religion, although within a few years their scope was broadened to include social and scientific problems.[13] A typical series was the one delivered during the winter of 1876–1877. Lectures on Jonathan Edwards, William Ellery Channing, and Theodore Parker were delivered by Francis Tiffany, Clay McCauley, and D. A. Wasson, respectively. Francis Abbot lectured on "The Scientific Method in Religion"; Frothingham spoke on

10. F. R. A., *First Annual Report, 1868,* pp. 6–7.
11. C. W. Wendte, *The Wider Fellowship,* I, 222–224.
12. F. R. A., *Proceedings, 1871,* pp. 11–12.
13. F. R. A., *Proceedings, 1875,* pp. 8–9.

"Jesus"; Minot Savage, the young utilitarian, dealt with "Immoral Religion and Irreligious Morality"; Professor Alpheus Hyatt expounded his evolutionary hypothesis concerning "Old Age in the Race and in the Individual"; William R. Alger spoke on "The Laboring Classes and the Ruling Classes; or How the World is to be Redeemed"; Professor E. S. Morse gave an illustrated lecture "Concerning Evolution"; and John W. Chadwick concluded the series with a talk on "Emanuel Swedenborg." [14] For the first few years the lectures excited considerable interest and were well attended. As the novelty of the free religious position wore off, however, and disagreements divided the Association, the maintenance of the lectures became a burden, and they were abandoned in 1878.

In order to gain a clearer picture of the religious situation and to consolidate the radical position Secretary Potter entered into extensive correspondence with rationalist groups not represented in the Association. Friendly sentiments were exchanged with Keshub Chunder Sen, leader of the Brahmoist movement in India, who hoped for the formation of a vast theistic brotherhood, of which the Brahmo-Somaj and the Free Religious Association would form the basis. Potter was obliged to reply that his organization was not a church and did not have a creed, even a theistic one, so that he was compelled to decline any coöperation beyond a friendly exchange of sentiments and mutual encouragement. [15] In all of its contacts with other groups the Association could not enter into any vital relationships without impairing the perfect freedom of opinion of some elements of its membership, which effectively prevented it from ever joining or leading an aggressive crusade for rationalistic religion.

Had the Association been less sensitive on the subject it might have strengthened the contacts that already existed between its leaders and the humanistic theists of England. In its broader contours the religious situation in that country was remarkably similar to that in the United States. The last of the civil disabilities placed upon Catholics and dissenters had been removed by the middle of the nineteenth century. The existence of an established church had not prevented the rapid growth and diversification of denominations and sects of all kinds, Calvinist, evan-

---

14. F. R. A., *Proceedings, 1877*, p. 13.
15. F. R. A., *Proceedings, 1868*, p. 5; *Proceedings, 1871*, pp. 13–14.

gelical, and radical. On the contrary, the preservation of the establishment seemed to place a premium upon freedom and tolerance, while at the same time it assured the maintenance of that great reservoir of churchly sophistication and learning that was so intimately connected with English culture of the day. This was particularly true of the Broad Church party, whose latitudinarian theological views upon occasion approached closely to those of the Unitarians.[16]

On the left wing of English Christianity Unitarianism was passing through much the same doctrinal evolution that has been found in American Unitarianism. The scripture rationalism of Locke that had established itself in Unitarian thinking had given way to transcendental idealism introduced from Germany by Coleridge. But this transformation had been accomplished under the leadership of the most influential English Unitarians, James Martineau and J. J. Tayler, and it was attended by little of the bitterness or controversy that characterized the process on the other side of the Atlantic. In the era of evolutionary thought, after the publication of *The Origin of Species*, the requirements of rational theism led the most restless English thinkers beyond the recognized bounds of Christianity to much the same position being taken at the same time by the humanistic theists of the Free Religious Association. Professor Francis W. Newman, brother of the Catholic, John Henry Newman, and Frances Power Cobbe wrote extensively on behalf of a rational religion that drew its inspiration from universal human experience.[17]

While English Unitarianism felt these stresses it did not react in the direction of doctrinal exclusiveness. No creed or test was proposed to define the limits of fellowship, and the views of its preachers ranged all the way from traditional Socinianism to the religion of humanity. Moncure D. Conway, the young American liberal who went to England to plead the Union cause during the Civil War, remained there in close contact with Unitarians and theists to the end of the century. In 1864 Conway was invited to become minister of South Place Chapel, a non-sectarian church established during the French Revolution by an American Uni-

16. Goblet d'Alviella, *Contemporary Religious Thought*, pp. 63–67.
17. See F. W. Newman, *Phases of Faith* (London, 1850); *The Soul: Its Sorrows and Its Aspirations* (8th ed., London, 1868). F. P. Cobbe, *Broken Lights: An Inquiry into the Present Condition and Future Prospects of Religious Faith* (Boston, 1864).

versalist, Elhanan Winchester. Conway's predecessor, William Johnson Fox, famous for his political reform activities, had passed through Unitarianism to a humanized theism, and had furthermore antagonized his Unitarian colleagues by his unorthodox social views. Nevertheless, Conway was warmly welcomed by the Unitarians, who invited him upon his arrival to attend their ministerial conference. He found them discussing precisely the same problem that was to divide the American Unitarians a year later. Martineau was maintaining that the terms Lord and Savior had no meaning for modern Christians, since these terms had been selected to designate a conception of Christ's messianic mission that retained no value for an age which had come to think of Christ's influence as operating on earth and in history, rather than in heaven. Conway recorded the fact that he was the only one present to endorse Martineau's views fully, yet the Unitarians remained friendly in spite of his radicalism.[18]

Because of the absence of Unitarian doctrinal tests the radical English religious thinkers were free to form their associations as they wished. Thus while Conway drew steadily away from the body of Unitarians, his friend F. W. Newman returned to them, and eventually took again formally the name of Unitarian that he had abandoned for many years. At the same time, Conway's anthology of sacred writings representative of the great world religions came to be widely used in Unitarian and non-sectarian churches in place of the traditional readings from the Bible.[19] In 1878 Conway and W. K. Clifford organized the Association of Liberal Thinkers, which was intended to serve the cause of European religious radicalism after the fashion of the Free Religious Association. Conway was in close contact with the American radicals, and his statement of principles for the new organization indicated how closely radical thinking in England paralleled that in America.[20] One congress of the Association was held, at which

18. Goblet d'Alviella, *Contemporary Religious Thought,* p. 96. Moncure D. Conway, *Autobiography, Memories and Experiences of Moncure D. Conway* (2 vols., London, 1904), II, 41–42.

19. Goblet d'Alviella, *Contemporary Religious Thought,* p. 88. Conway, *Autobiography,* II, 298–302. *The Sacred Anthology: A Book of Ethnical Scriptures* (New York, 1874).

20. The Association adopted the following program: "1. The scientific study of religious phenomena. 2. The collection and diffusion of information concerning religious movements throughout the world. 3. The emancipation of mankind from the spirit of superstition. 4. Fellowship among liberal thinkers of all races. 5. The promotion of culture, progress, and moral welfare of mankind, and of whatever

T. H. Huxley was elected president. The death of Clifford in the following year removed the person who might have kept the organization alive. The other leaders concluded that since ample opportunities of public teaching through periodicals and the lecture platform were available to them no further benefit was likely to be derived from organization. Thus within twelve months English radicals reached the conclusion that their American colleagues avoided for many years.

Within the United States contact was established with liberal groups throughout the country. The General Association of German Independent Congregations, at convention in Wisconsin in 1868, voted to coöperate with the Free Religious Association and urged its members to join and contribute to it. The North American Turner-Bund also approved the Association's principles.[21] Many members of the Association belonged to the Twenty-eighth Congregational Society of Boston, Theodore Parker's old church, and relations with that group were extremely close. By 1871 several Radical Clubs modeled on the Association had sprung up in the Northeast and Midwest.[22] These groups, formed independently of the Association, provided obvious material out of which to weld together a nationwide free religious organization; or might have, had not many members feared the sectarian tendencies in such a policy. In their opinion free religion must be left to work its way in the world of ideas, receiving concrete formulation in organization only where local conditions caused natural crystallization. The leaders accepted this view in the early years, while the memory of their struggle with organized Unitarianism was still fresh. By 1880, however, when it was evident that the intransigent individualism of many members had become a fetish which would destroy the vitality of the organization if it were not rooted out, a vigorous effort was made by the activists to commit the Association to a more positive program; but in vain.

The moving spirit in the Free Religious Association, within the limits of movement permitted, was William J. Potter. Until his death in 1894 Potter literally held the Association together,

in any form of religion may tend towards that end. 6. Membership in this Association shall leave each individual responsible for his own opinion alone, and in no degree affect his relations with other associations." Conway, *Autobiography*, II, 352–355.

21. F. R. A., *Proceedings, 1869*, pp. 8–9, 18–19.
22. F. R. A., *Proceedings, 1871*, p. 12.

and with his passing the first and most important phase of the Association's history came to a close. No other member was so closely identified with its work as he, and to recount its activities during that period is practically to record the biography of Potter. With the other leaders it was not so. The work of Frothingham was chiefly identified with his liberal society in New York. Felix Adler deserted the Free Religious Association for his own Ethical Culture Society. Minot Savage occupied Unitarian pulpits in Boston and New York throughout his life, making his chief contribution in the liberalization of Unitarianism. Francis Abbot, who was chiefly instrumental in the formation of the Association, had a remarkable career outside of it, which requires some attention.

As Abbot's radicalism grew upon him it was inevitable that a sizable portion of his Dover, New Hampshire, parish should refuse to follow him, although apparently a considerable majority were swept along by the intense earnestness and convincing logic of the young preacher. His inability to reconcile the findings of modern knowledge with the fundamentals of Christianity as he understood them, however, forced him to resign his pastorate in the spring of 1868. The resignation was accepted, although the Society voted to retain him for a year as its preacher. Abbot would accept only upon condition that the Unitarian society dissolve itself, or that a separate Independent society be organized. The latter course was followed, and Abbot preached his first sermon to the new society in American Hall, Dover, on April 26, 1868. On the following day the Unitarian society voted, 53 to 46, to give the use of their meeting house alternately to "each of the two divisions of the society." But the forty-six conservative Unitarians refused to accept the decision and applied to the courts for an injunction forbidding Abbot's use of the building. Counsel for Abbot's group decided to fight the case on the ground that they constituted a majority of the original society, in spite of the fact that their organization as an Independent society was practically, if not legally, complete. Abbot objected to such legal strategy on conscientious grounds, and when his friends insisted upon fighting the case on those terms, he resigned the Independent pulpit as well. That should have ended the matter; but the court action was continued, and eventually the Supreme Court of New Hampshire handed down a sweeping injunction forbidding

Abbot, a non-Christian, to occupy the pulpit of the Unitarian society as long as any member of that society should object.[23]

The central figure of the famous Dover Case thus gained something of a national reputation, and opportunity soon presented itself for the use of his talents on a wider scale. Mr. David R. Locke, of Toledo, Ohio, proprietor of the *Toledo Blade* and creator of the Reverend Petroleum Vesuvius Nasby, whose syndicated column was widely read at that time, appears to have harbored secret leanings towards rational religion. Locke had earlier joined the Methodist Church, apparently to relieve the fears of his prospective mother-in-law. He was admittedly not a very sincere convert, and slightingly referred to himself as a pillar of the church—"an outside support." [24] The Unitarian society in Toledo had attempted repeatedly during the months following Abbot's resignation to persuade the latter to accept its pulpit. Now Locke came forward with the offer to finance a weekly journal of free religion, sustaining all costs for the first year, up to $3,000. Albert E. Macomber and Abbot would be joint proprietors with him, Abbot having sole editorial charge. He would receive no salary, for the plan was contingent upon his acceptance of the call from the Toledo Unitarian society. Abbot agreed on condition that the Unitarians drop their sectarian connection and become an Independent society. To make his position clear he preached a series of sermons in Toledo during the summer of 1869, in which he sketched the fundamentals of free religion and discussed the defects of Christianity. The society was convinced, dissolved itself, and reformed as the First Independent Society of Toledo.[25] On November 1 prospectuses announcing a new journal of radical religion were sent out, and on January 1, 1870, the first issue of *The Index* appeared.

In his prospectus Abbot announced that *The Index* would have the positive objective of increasing genuine religion by developing a nobler spirit and higher purpose in the individual and in society; negatively, it would seek to increase freedom by destroying spiritual slavery. "Without limiting itself to any of the great reformatory movements of the time, it proposes to work for them

23. *The Index,* II (Dec. 2, 1871), 379.
24. Cyril Clemens, *Petroleum Vesuvius Nasby* (Webster Groves, Mo., 1936), pp. 9, 12.
25. *Universal Religion,* XI, no. 9 (Dec., 1903. Memorial number in honor of the late F. E. Abbot), 153–155. Abbot, *The Inside History of the Index Association* . . . (Cambridge, Mass., 1873), p. 1.

all in the most efficient way, by fostering the *spirit of reform*, and by uprooting every conservative prejudice by which reform is checked. Uncompromising, fearless, radical, it will put faith in ideas, and work for them openly, regardless of all consequences." Nevertheless, every phase of earnest thought would receive a hearing—atheism and transcendentalism, positivism as well as spiritualism, free religion, Christianity, and materialism. In its editorial policy the journal was to be frankly the organ of free religion, but it promised to be fair to all other systems of thought. It would pay no deference to the authority of Bible, Church, or Christ, but would rest solely on the sanction of right reason and good conscience. It promised to accept every certified result of science, philosophy, and historical criticism.[26]

The first few issues of *The Index* carried Abbot's Fifty Affirmations prominently displayed. Comparable to Luther's ninety-five theses, only better, according to Colonel Higginson, the Fifty Affirmations were short statements defining the nature of religion as the universal expression of human personality, with its peculiar variations in each of the great religions, and its final formulation in free religion.[27] The Unitarians twitted Abbot with having left their denomination because of its brief creed, only to produce one of fifty articles himself. It was necessary for him to insist that the Affirmations represented his personal views alone, and in no sense committed his colleagues in the Free Religious Association. The first group of articles concerned the nature of pure, or universal, religion. (1) "Religion is the effort of man to perfect himself." (2) "The root of religion is universal human nature." (3) "Historical religions are all one, in virtue of this common root." (4) "Historical religions are all different, in virtue of their different historical origin and development." (6) "The universal element is the same in all historical religions; the special element is peculiar to each of them."

The second group of articles indicated the relation of Judaism to Christianity. Judaism had developed the idea of an earthly "kingdom of heaven" ruled over by the Messiah. It was to be a world-wide temporal and spiritual empire established by the miraculous intervention of Jehovah. Jesus came announcing himself to be this Messiah, expecting the miraculous consummation

26. *The Index*, I (Jan. 1, 1870), 5.
27. *The Index*, I (Jan. 1, 1870), 1.

of the prophecy (Articles 10–17). (18) "As a preacher of purely spiritual truth, Jesus probably stands at the head of all the great religious teachers of the past." (19) "As claimant of the Messianic crown, and as founder of Christianity as a distinct historical religion, Jesus shared the spirit of an unenlightened age, and stands on the same level with Gautama or Mohammed."

Christianity, according to Abbot, was simply the complete development of Judaism. It taught that Jesus was the Messiah, and that the individual must confess this to achieve salvation. The Roman Catholic Church and theology were built upon that confession; they were its logical development into a religion of authority (Articles 21–27). (28) "Protestantism is the gradual disintegration of Christianity, whether regarded theologically or ecclesiastically, under the influence of the free spirit of protest against authority." (29) " 'Liberal Christianity'—that is, democratic autocracy in religion—is the highest development of the free spirit of protest against authority which is possible within the Christian church. It is, at the same time, the lowest possible development of faith in the Christ—a return to the Christian Confession in its crudest and least developed form."

Under the head of free religion Abbot inconsistently outlined his own brand of theism. He had actually summarized free religion in his first articles on the nature of religion itself. (35) "Free Religion is emancipation from the outward law, and voluntary obedience to the inward law." (36) "The great faith or moving power of Free Religion is faith in man as a progressive being." (37) "The great ideal end of Free Religion is the perfection or complete development of man—the race serving the individual, the individual serving the race." (38) "The great practical means of Free Religion is the integral, continuous and universal education of man." (39) "The great law of Free Religion is the still small voice of the private soul." (40) "The great peace of Free Religion is spiritual oneness with the infinite One." The emphasis of Abbot's religion was unquestionably humanistic, but its values were guaranteed and its motivation assured by man's relation to the infinite One. The Fifty Affirmations were elucidated by essays in the first seven issues of the magazine, the seven sermons preached to the Toledo Unitarian society in order to convert it to Free Religion.

The bulk of the material in *The Index* during the first few years was from the pen of Abbot himself. The Free Religious

Association maintained a column under the charge of Secretary Potter, and other leaders, especially Frothingham and Higginson, were frequent contributors. But the backbone of the paper consisted of Abbot's essays and editorials. The essays were frequently sermons previously read to the Independent society. He received a salary of only $2,000 from the society on condition that he be exempted from pastoral work. *The Index* paid him no salary at all until October, 1871, when the Independent society found itself able to raise Abbot's ministerial salary only with the greatest difficulty.[28]

Locke and Macomber renewed the terms of publication for a second year, but in April, 1871, the Index Association was incorporated to assume publication and relieve them of the expense. Stock at ten dollars a share was sold up to the amount of $50,000 in order to acquire the journal from the original proprietors. The purchaser of stock was to pay 10 percent of its value annually, however, rather than the full sum outright. This unwise provision resulted in wholesale delinquency in later years.[29] By October, 1871, 2,100 copies were being printed weekly, and in June, 1872, 4,900 copies,[30] of which some 4,500 represented paid subscriptions. An intensely earnest man, Abbot demanded of his associates an equal devotion to the cause to which he was giving his life without thought of recompense. Yet he appears to have been a singularly poor judge of character, and to have possessed to a remarkable degree the ability to antagonize his associates. Differences of policy with his printer and advertising agent led to charges against them of unscrupulousness by Abbot and of mismanagement on his part by Bateson, the printer, and by Asa K. Butts, the agent. The documents presented by Abbot and printed in *The Inside History of the Index Association* seem to support his charges, although Bateson and Butts were able to persuade the Board of Directors to remove Abbot from the business managership, March 14, 1873. Abbot promptly resigned from the editorship and passed the whole matter along to the annual meeting of the stockholders in June. A majority of the stock was held by members and friends of the Free Religious Association, who accepted Abbot's version of the difficulty. Colonel

28. Abbot, *The Inside History of the Index Association*, pp. 22, 52–53.
29. Abbot, *The Inside History of the Index Association*, p. 2.
30. Index Association Record Book, in the handwriting of Abbot and others. Pages unnumbered. Abbot papers.

Higginson came to Toledo armed to vote a majority of the stock by proxy, and Abbot was reinstated, to the discomfiture of his opponents.[31]

The "Index Troubles" were given considerable notoriety by journalistic enemies, and the affair cost the magazine several hundred subscribers, besides ruining its promising financial outlook. It was significant that Butts thought the possibilities for a radical anti-Christian journal promising enough to warrant high-pressure methods of promotion. The challenge to the dominant religious system had assumed such proportions that this shrewd adventurer could envision himself "the Henry C. Bowen of *The Index.*" [32] After Abbot had regained control of the paper it seemed desirable to remove it to Boston, where it would receive closer support from its friends. Abbot continued as editor from 1873 to 1880. Although the quality of the paper constantly improved, it was never able to earn its expenses. With the tenth annual assessment on the stock an additional issue would have been necessary had not Abbot become completely discouraged. *The Index* was made over to the Free Religious Association in 1880 without cost, with the proviso that the Association continue to publish it in the interests of free religion.[33] Examination of the books of the Index Association shows that the chief financial supporters of the magazine during the years of Abbot's management were John M. Forbes, William C. Gannett, A. M. Howland, Elizur Wright, J. C. Haynes, and Samuel E. Sewell, all of Boston; Samuel L. Hill, of Florence, Massachusetts; Arethusa Hall, of Northampton; Mrs. F. W. Christern, of New York City; O. B. Frothingham; A. C. Gurley, of Pulaski, New York; Mary Shannon, of Newton; and A. E. Macomber, of Toledo.[34]

31. Index Association Record Book.

32. Abbot, *The Inside History of the Index Association,* p. 25.

33. Index Association Record Book.

34. Before 1880 *The Index* was entirely the work of Abbot, and was designed to spread free religion as he conceived it. To include the journal among the periodicals of transcendentalism, as does Professor Gohdes (*The Periodicals of American Transcendentalism,* pp. 229–254) is to misrepresent the dominant rationalism of the free religious movement. Abbot's vigorous attack upon the intuitionalists in 1877 did not, as Gohdes implies, indicate a reverse from transcendentalism. Abbot was never a transcendentalist. The germs of his scientific theism, a rationalistic religion, may be found in his earliest essays, written during the Civil War. In his Horticultural Hall Lecture of 1871, on the "Intuitional and Scientific Schools of Free Religion," discussed in Chapter II, Abbot denied the validity of the transcendentalist approach by insisting that the use of the scientific method was the only means of attaining intellectual truth, whether one was study-

After *The Index* had passed to the Association in 1880 it was edited by Potter and Underwood. Under their management the magazine remained easily the finest liberal religious journal in America. Although the circulation increased slightly the project was still far from self-supporting, and much of the financial assistance which the Association received was absorbed in its maintenance. When it became evident that a journal of high quality dedicated to free religion could not be sustained without retrenching on the other activities of the Association it was decided in 1886 to abandon *The Index*.[35] With the last issue in 1886 remaining subscribers were transferred to *Unity*, a liberal Unitarian publication in Chicago, or to the *Open Court*. The passing of *The Index* left free religion without an organ of its own. Morse's *Radical* had expired in 1872. Potter had sponsored a *Radical Review* in New Bedford which survived for less than a year (May, 1877—February, 1878). In the same year in which Abbot founded *The Index* Edward C. Towne, who had gone to Chicago, launched the *Examiner*, "a monthly review of religious and humane questions." The *Examiner* also was unable to maintain itself for a year (1870–1871). With the loss of its journals the one chance that free religion might establish itself as a distinct religious movement vanished.

In addition to the periodical, the convention was a favorite method of spreading free religious ideas. Conventions in cities other than Boston were held under the auspices of the Association almost annually after 1871. By 1885, when the last convention was held, New York, Chicago, Philadelphia, Detroit, Albany, Syracuse, Cincinnati, and Indianapolis, as well as smaller eastern cities, had been visited. The typical convention comprised three or four public meetings addressed by the officers or other leaders of the Association at which the meaning of free religion would be discussed. Besides these official conventions sponsored by the Association individual members did much lecturing on their own initiative. Parker Pillsbury and B. F. Underwood made extensive lecture tours throughout the country.[36]

From the contacts thus established it soon became evident that an extensive revolt against the Christian churches was in progress

ing natural phenomena, philosophy, or religion. The disgust of the transcendentalists with *The Index* was not so much due to its propaganda methods as to their fear of the results of Abbot's "philosophized scientific method."

35. F. R. A., *Proceedings, 1887,* pp. 8–10.

36. *The Index*, II (April 15 and 22, 1871), 116, 124.

during the three decades following the Civil War. The great decision facing the Free Religious Association was whether to attempt to organize and lead this revolt in accordance with its own conception of rational and non-sectarian theism. The leaders of the Association were acquainted with the spectacular success of Keshub Chunder Sen in enlarging the Brahmo-Somaj of Calcutta into a national theistic society with local groups scattered throughout India.[37] Their task would in some respects be less difficult than his, for it was clear that many Americans had already abandoned allegiance to the Christian churches and were spontaneously organizing themselves locally in order to give expression to the new rationalistic impulse. These groups called themselves variously Radical, Liberal, or Free Religious Clubs. They were to be found in most of the larger cities of the Northeast and Middle West as well as in many smaller communities. To a remarkable degree they were motivated by the same spirit that underlay the Free Religious Association. The unanimity with which their constitutions emphasized the importance of free discussion and investigation indicated the widespread feeling of the time that the churches were hostile or indifferent to the current problems that occupied men's minds. They proposed to deal impartially with scientific and moral as well as with religious questions. They were motivated by the desire to establish the authority of reason and right through the search for truth in the scientific spirit. And most of them dedicated themselves to social reform in the interest of progress and equal rights.[38] The Free Religious Association possessed a personnel capable of furnishing national leadership for religious radicalism should the Association wish to take the initiative.

Over the question of founding local societies of free religion after the manner of the churches, however, there was much dis-

37. For an account of the Brahmo-Somaj see J. N. Farquhar, *Modern Religious Movements in India* (New York, 1915), pp. 29–74. Acquaintance with Christianity through the work of missionaries and the influence of the British civil service played a large part in the formation of the Brahmoist movement. But Keshub Chunder Sen and his followers distinguished between Christ's moral teaching and the messianic claims advanced by his disciples. These Indians, needless to say, had no interest in Christ as the Messiah.

38. Such groups had been formed in Providence, Saint Louis, Indianapolis, Syracuse, Toledo, Pittsburgh, and many smaller communities. *The Index*, I (Jan. 15, 1870), 3; I (April 2, 1870), 7; I (July 16, 1870), 5; I (August 27, 1870), 3; I (Sept. 24, 1870), 4; II, 84, 86; III, 115, 211, 213; IV, 358, 362, 468; n.s., II, 509. Outside of New England the interest in rational religion was confined almost exclusively to New York and the old Northwest.

agreement. The question was not settled conclusively until 1894, when the vitality of the movement had been so far spent that the decision to organize local groups organically related to the Boston Association was meaningless.[39] Those favoring local organization were at first the humanitarian reformers[40] who wished to identify free religion with philanthropic work. Abbot and Potter, who originally had doubts as to whether the Association could constitutionally pursue an active religious program, realized by 1880 that such an effort would be the only means of saving free religion from sterility, and they used all their influence to convert the Association to a policy of religious organization. On the other hand, a number of members, especially those who lived in Boston, wished their organization to remain merely a platform for the expression of liberal ideas. Their position can be understood only in the light of the extreme individualism of the time. It was a widely held idea that organization killed the spirit. Samuel Johnson in 1879 was lamenting the tendency of radicalism to rely upon numbers, utilities, and outward forces rather than upon individual power and spirit.[41] Such a typically transcendentalist attitude was shared by many of the rank and file in the Association.

The problem of the relation of the Association to similar liberal religious groups first arose in 1870, and the Executive Committee decided that the Association was an organization of individuals only. Since formal coöperation with other groups might infringe upon the views of some members the Association could not even empower delegates to represent it in joint functions.[42] At the same time that this decision was announced, Secretary Potter outlined a broad program of social and religious activity which the Association could inaugurate by itself.[43] However, he did not make it clear how it would be possible to do more than talk about reform if the constitutional restraint upon all action contrary to the private opinions of members was to be scrupulously observed. Three years later the committee indicated that the opinions of members should be respected, by deciding that none of the suggestions for spreading free religious institutions would be acted upon. These suggestions had included the actual founding of

39. F. R. A., *Proceedings, 1894,* pp. 4–6.
40. See Chapter VII.
41. Johnson, *Lectures,* p. 127.
42. F. R. A., *Proceedings, 1870,* pp. 8–9.
43. See Chapter VII.

Free Religious Associations in other localities, the extending of
financial aid to local preachers who expounded free religious principles, or merely the sending out of paid lecturers to spread radical ideas. The committee agreed that the Association should confine itself to periodicals and its own lecture platform.[44]

The care with which the Association protected the opinions of
its members was occasionally carried to absurd lengths. The individualistic element reflected in the revolt against Unitarianism
now reigned supreme. At the Annual Meeting in 1876 the problem
of representing the Association in the Centennial Congress of
Liberals arose. The Congress was to be composed of representatives of Abbot's Liberal Leagues, which had been organized to
frustrate a movement of the early 'seventies to secure a Christian
amendment to the Federal Constitution.[45] The Executive Committee decided it would violate the principles of the Association to be
officially represented at the Congress. A unanimous resolution was
passed, however, demanding that the Centennial Exposition be
open to the public on Sundays, since the Exposition was a national project, and Sunday was the only free day for many working people. Presumably some members had abstained from voting
on this resolution, for immediately R. P. Hallowell and Sidney
Morse called attention to the inconsistency between the resolution
and the principle that had determined the committee to refuse
coöperation with the Liberal Congress. William C. Gannett replied that such strict construction would logically limit the Association to mere discussion, forbidding even a resolution to sum up
the sense of opinion on any subject. C. E. Pratt observed that
since the problem was moral and social rather than credal, the
Association had the right to express an opinion. Bronson Alcott
then interjected some delphic observations on the metaphysics of
passing a resolution which were scarcely calculated to throw light
on the immediate problem. Addison Davis brought the discussion
back to the practical level by replying to Pratt that the matter
was credal: the resolution would commit the Association to the
creed of Anti-Sabbatarianism. Others joined him in branding the
resolution as essentially dogmatic. Apparently they felt themselves caught in the meshes of their own principles. Finally Hallo-

44. F. R. A., *Proceedings, 1873*, p. 12.
45. See Chapter VI. *Report of the Centennial Congress of Liberals, and Organization of the National Liberal League, at Philadelphia, on the Fourth of July,
1876* (Boston, 1876), pp. 7–18.

well suggested that, since so many members had departed, the Association ought not to be committed either way, and the resolution originally passed unanimously was quietly tabled.[46]

Little organized activity could be expected from an Association which guarded the individual opinions of its members as carefully as this. Already its program had become fixed, with the Annual Meetings, courses of lectures, conventions in other cities, and the circulation of tracts and other literature. By 1879 the Association had lost much of its vitality. Receipts, which had reached $2,600 in 1875,[47] now dropped to $800, an amount insufficient to print the Annual Proceedings and maintain the Horticultural Hall Lectures, which were consequently suspended.[48] Ill health had forced Frothingham to resign the presidency in 1878.[49] Felix Adler was chosen to succeed him, and with the change in leadership came a new drive to galvanize the Association. Abbot and Potter were now convinced that an active policy was the only way to save free religion, and they sponsored the appointment of a committee to prepare a plan for the more effective presentation of free religious principles.[50]

Adler agreed that reformation was necessary, and on assuming the presidency outlined his own ideas on the development of free religious organization. Most important for its maintenance he considered a system of education, starting with moral and ethical training for the young and continuing up to the professional level. Such training formed the basis of his Society for Ethical Culture in New York. A School for the Science of Religion would be needed to train free religious leaders, and until one could be established Adler suggested that funds be raised to endow chairs of the Science of Religion, rational ethics, and social science in existing universities. A journal which would be the official organ of the Association was also needed. Some method of establishing local societies organically related to the parent group must be worked out. Finally, the Association must make up its mind to take an immediate interest in the advancement of human welfare and concern itself with the problems of poverty, industrialism, and property.[51] Abbot and F. A. Hinckley heartily endorsed

46. F. R. A., *Proceedings, 1876*, pp. 13–14, 20–23.
47. F. R. A., *Proceedings, 1875*, p. 7.
48. F. R. A., *Proceedings, 1879*, p. 7.
49. F. R. A., *Proceedings, 1878*, p. 8.
50. F. R. A., *Proceedings, 1879*, pp. 7–14.
51. F. R. A., *Proceedings, 1879*, pp. 44–53.

Adler's proposals. Both agreed that the time had come for national organization. Unless the Association could overcome the spirit of selfish individualism that had characterized its first twelve years, they agreed that it might as well disband.[52]

The committee on organization reported a plan of increased activity at the Annual Meeting in 1880, which, however, fell far short of the expectations of the leaders. It urged the "encouragement" of local free religious societies and Sunday schools, the employment of lecturers by the Association in order to hold more frequent conventions, and the enlargement of the publishing medium both by supporting a journal and by producing books for juvenile instruction. Acting upon these suggestions the Executive Committee raised $1,000 by private solicitation to employ a general agent who should arrange lecture engagements, collect statistics, and "aid" in the formation of local societies. It was sheer coincidence that the Index Association found itself facing a financial crisis at this moment. After ten years of labor Abbot was still unable to make the venture self-supporting, and was forced to concede that it would require more than the efforts of one man to produce a successful weekly journal. *The Index* was transferred to the Free Religious Association, thus bringing to the support of the new program a magazine of distinguished reputation.[53]

In carrying into effect even a modified reform program the committee encountered strong opposition within the Association. The exact nature of the coöperation which should be extended through the general agent to the local societies became the central problem, and the matter was debated for a year without decision. At the Annual Meeting in May, 1881, Mrs. Anna Garlin Spencer[54] proposed that local correspondents be appointed in each state to gather information on legal restrictions upon religious liberty, religious influences in public education, and the possibilities of forming local free religious societies. She also pro-

52. F. R. A., *Proceedings, 1879*, pp. 58–63, 64–68.
53. F. R. A., Annual Proceedings, 1880, *The Index*, n.s., I (July 1, 1880), 10–11.
54. The Spencers were among the most prominent members of the Association in the later years of its activity. William H. Spencer remained in the Unitarian pulpit and was influential in modifying the older Unitarian orthodoxy. His wife, Anna Garlin Spencer, who deserves a place among the great reformers of the nineteenth century, devoted herself indefatigably to preaching, education, philanthropy, and various reforms. As the vitality of the Free Religious Association waned she transferred her activities to the Ethical Culture movement. See the sketch of Mrs. Spencer in the *Dictionary of American Biography*.

posed that State Auxiliaries to the Association be formed. The appointment of local correspondents was approved, but the idea of Auxiliaries smacked too much of ecclesiasticism, and after much debate the proposal was referred to the Executive Committee, where it was quietly pigeon-holed.[55] At the same meeting a committee of five, headed by Mrs. Spencer, was entrusted with the thorny problem of local organization. The aim of the committee was to please all parties so far as possible.[56] It recommended that the Association collect information on the prospects of liberalism in different localities. Where the conditions seemed favorable the Association should urge the formation of a free religious society, and it might even aid financially in the preliminary organization. But there should be no organic relation between the local society and the parent group. These recommendations were unanimously accepted at the Annual Meeting in 1882.[57]

Felix Adler had proposed his plan of action in 1879, and had waited for three years while the Association debated the merits of home rule and the potential dangers of sectarianism in a national free religious organization. Adler's patience was exhausted by 1882, and at the Annual Meeting of that year he resigned from the Association. Although he remained heartily in favor of the principles of the free religious platform he was disgusted with the scrupulousness of the Association's policy. The idea of the sympathy of religions was excellent, he believed, but if carried too far there was danger that one might lose his own distinctive beliefs, thus undermining the source of religious action. Adler's personal creed of agnosticism placed supreme emphasis upon benevolent action, and he measured all religious professions against that standard. It was time for the free religionists to stop talking and act. "What has Boston done for the honor of our principles," demanded Adler. "What great charitable movement has found its source here among those who maintain the principle of freedom in religion? What living thing for the good of mankind, for the perfecting of morality among yourselves and others, has emanated within the last twenty years from the Free Religious circles of this city? I say to you, friends, . . . these annual meetings will not answer." [58]

55. F. R. A., Proceedings, 1881, *The Index*, n.s., I (June 9, 1881), 590–591.
56. "Report of the Special Committee . . .," *The Index*, n.s., II (April 13, 1882), 487–489.
57. F. R. A., Proceedings, 1882, *The Index*, n.s., II (June 8, 1882), 582–585.
58. F. R. A., Proceedings, 1882, *The Index*, n.s., II (June 22, 1882), 606–607.

The Association was not to be moved out of its comfortable ways by Adler's attack. It was found in 1883 that special financial efforts were necessary to save *The Index*, and all other activity was sacrificed to keep the journal alive.[59] By 1884 the Executive Committee admitted for the first time that the function of the Association was now conceded by all hands to be the passive one of disseminating ideas.[60] *The Index* was given up in 1886, but no other form of activity was found to replace it. The Association was slowly atrophying.

At the Columbian Exposition at Chicago in 1893 there convened the first World Parliament of Religions. Free religious leaders looked upon it as the product of their labors in behalf of the common principles which bound all religions together. Twenty years before, in 1872, Secretary Potter had predicted with remarkable foresight the day when such a gathering could take place. He had said:

Some of us here may live to see the day when there shall be a World's Convention, in London, or perhaps in Boston, or San Francisco, of representatives from all the great religions of the globe— coming together in a spirit of mutual respect, confidence, and amity, for common conference on what may be for the best good of all; not to make a common creed by patching articles together from their respective faiths in which they might find themselves in agreement, but emancipated from all bondage to creed and sect, to join hands in a common effort to help mankind to higher truth and nobler living. It may be that the work of this Association will culminate in such a World's Convention.[61]

The twenty-sixth Annual Meeting of the Free Religious Association in 1893 was held in Chicago at the Parliament its leader had predicted. The effective work of the Association was completed, and it had come to the Exposition in a sense to view the results of its labors. That representatives of the great world religions met together in amicable terms could not be denied. Abbot noted, however, that each claimed for his own faith the status of universal religion, and he left the Exposition convinced

59. F. R. A., Proceedings, 1884, *The Index,* n.s., IV (June 5, 1884), 584–585.
60. F. R. A., Proceedings, 1884, *The Index,* n.s., IV (June 5, 1884), 585.
61. F. R. A., *Proceedings, 1872,* p. 15.

that the free religious movement had failed.[62] The prevailing sentiment, nevertheless, was one of mutual congratulation. B. F. Underwood informed the Association that it saw in the Parliament the tangible results of its work, and that it could now disband in triumph.[63] The true estimate seems to fall somewhere between the two views. Sectarianism was by no means overcome, but the Free Religious Association had made an important contribution to the liberalizing process which had worked deep into religion in the later nineteenth century.

62. F. R. A., *Proceedings, 1893,* p. 7. Abbot, *Outlines of the Liberal Religious Situation* (Tacoma, 1895), p. 6.
63. F. R. A., *Proceedings, 1893,* pp. 76–80.

## THE RELIGION OF HUMANITY

THE Free Religious movement was inevitably shaped to some extent by the character of the Christian churches in the mid-nineteenth century. Within the multiple sects in America could be discerned a rapidly disintegrating Calvinism; an unsophisticated Protestant evangelicalism; a rapidly growing Catholicism, confined within fairly strict nationality and class lines; a small and undistinguished Episcopal church utterly unable to sustain a Broad Church movement; and numerically insignificant Unitarian and Universalist churches preoccupied with their "pale negations." Among the sects there was no church of both preëminent national influence and high intellectual tradition able to absorb and represent on behalf of Christianity the best thought of the day. Nevertheless, religious and social morality were almost completely dominated by the traditional Christian concepts.

Against this Christian monopoly over respectable intellectual patterns the two decades after Appomattox saw a widespread rebellion. The Emersonian transcendentalists had launched the attack before the war with their pantheistic theology. The spirit of revolt quickly permeated down from the intellectual elite to the middle class, where it became a popular crusade, which has been named "the Religion of Humanity." [1] As a folk movement the Religion of Humanity has yet to receive intensive study, but it is evident that its ramifications ran deep into American society.[2] The inevitable unrest following the convulsions of civil conflict undoubtedly played its part in fomenting rebellion. At the root of the movement lay a growing disbelief in the adequacy of the Christian teachings. New sciences of an historical character, geology, anthropology, and paleontology, together with the application of the development hypothesis to biology, asked formid-

---

1. R. H. Gabriel, *The Course of American Democratic Thought* (New York, 1940), pp. 173–186.

2. For a factual account of the anti-religious movement in the late nineteenth century see Sidney Warren, *American Freethought, 1865–1914* (New York, 1943).

able questions difficult to answer within the framework of orthodoxy; and they provided new answers which seemed to require
basic readjustments in the Christian cosmology. The scientific
men appear to have felt the impact of the new ideas as quickly as
any. Robert Dale Owen reported the undoubtedly exaggerated
but nevertheless significant opinion of a Harvard professor in
1867 that three-fourths or more of the leading American scientists were admitted or silent infidels.[3] A rationalistic age has overlooked them in heaping scorn upon the few Agassizs who tailored
their science to fit their theology.

At the end of the century Francis Abbot was to look back upon
these years as the age of agnosticism.[4] In discarding the Christian
cosmology many Americans found no substitute to sustain their
spiritual values, and free religion proposed to offer such a substitute. Although it shared the revolt against Orthodoxy, much of
its effort was spent in attempting to shape the negative criticism
prevalent in the air into a positive and constructive religious
liberalism. Within its own ranks it had to combat such a natural
reaction to the unyielding formulas of the Christian theology as
was expressed by Richard P. Hallowell, a respectable Boston busi-
nessman, when he declared theology to be the enemy of pure,
undefiled religion. A true faith, he insisted, appeals to the conscience, heart, sympathy, and common intelligence of men, and
forgets speculative theology.[5] A more sophisticated but equally
earnest attack was launched by the influential scientist and historian, John W. Draper, who published in 1875 his *History of
the Conflict between Religion and Science.* The book ran through
several editions and was translated into nine languages.[6] After
reviewing the earlier phases of the conflict, which he traced from
medieval times, the tract concluded with a forecast of the final
battle which Draper believed was about to open. "As to the issue
of the coming conflict," he cried, "can anyone doubt? Whatever
is resting on fiction and fraud will be overthrown. Institutions
that organize impostures and spread delusions must show what
right they have to exist. Faith must render an account of herself
to Reason. Mysteries must give place to facts. Religion must

3. F. R. A., *Report of Addresses at a Meeting Held in Boston, May 30, 1867*
. . . (Boston, 1867), pp. 17–18.
4. Abbot, *The Way out of Agnosticism, or the Philosophy of Free Religion*
(Boston, 1890), pp. vii–xi.
5. F. R. A., *Proceedings at the First Annual Meeting . . . 1868* (Boston, 1868),
pp. 17–18.
6. See the sketch of Draper in the *Dictionary of American Biography.*

relinquish that imperious, that domineering position which she has so long maintained against Science. There must be absolute freedom for thought." [7]

Draper's book, then, was a prelude to the last act. Twenty years later the entire drama was to be surveyed in a book of a similar title: Andrew D. White's *History of the Warfare of Science with Theology in Christendom*.[8] White again recounted the unhappy story of narrow ecclesiastical intolerance, but it was no longer necessary to write with the same militancy. To all intents and purposes the battle had been won by science. Between the appearance of these two books the Religion of Humanity ate into the vitals of popular orthodoxy and destroyed many of the traditional elements of the Christian confession.

The extent and influence of cracker-barrel atheism in this postwar period can scarcely be estimated, but it is certain that the atheist became the great national bogy until replaced by the anarchist of the mid-'eighties. In the forms of agnosticism, materialism, positivism, and free-thought atheism received noisy, if limited, expression through press and platform. The Free Religious Association welcomed such partisans cordially at its meetings in the hope of improving their moral tone. The most distinguished of the materialists, Benjamin Franklin Underwood, became co-editor, with William J. Potter, of *The Index*, after its acquisition in 1880 by the Association from Abbot. Although agnosticism boasted impressive intellectual credentials in the writings of Herbert Spencer, its negative position made it an extremely unsatisfactory creed for thoughtful people. John Fiske, Spencer's leading disciple in America, went "through nature to God," [9] and almost alone among his contemporaries foresaw the outcome of the crusade when he wrote in 1875 that the God of the scientific philosopher was the same as that of the Christian, although shorn of the illegitimate dogmas by which theology had sought to make God comprehensible.[10] By the end of the century a large section of liberal Protestantism would admit the loss of vitality of many of its formulas, whether or not "illegitimate." Herbert Spencer himself lived to approve the theistic ver-

7. J. W. Draper, *History of the Conflict Between Religion and Science* (New York, 1875), p. 367.

8. A. D. White, *A History of the Warfare of Science with Theology in Christendom* (2 vols., New York, 1896).

9. John Fiske, *Through Nature to God* (Boston and New York, 1899).

10. John Fiske, *Outlines of Cosmic Philosophy* (2 vols., Boston, 1875), II, 416–423.

sion of his philosophy preached in America by Minot Savage and William J. Potter under the label of Cosmism.[11]

At a somewhat lower intellectual level anti-Christian activity was vigorously pushed. In March, 1869, Henry W. Bellows lectured in Washington, D. C., and in his audience sat a young government clerk named Lester Frank Ward. Ward found little of interest in the remarks of the leading orthodox Unitarian, and six days later he could be found attending a "strong and logical discourse" by B. F. Underwood on the problem of God, which he found much more to his liking.[12] The Sunday Lyceum of which Ward was a member held "free religious meetings," at which Christianity stood equally on its merits with "foeticide" and polygamy. Such pernicious activity among civil servants attracted the hostile comment of the press, and Ward led in the formation of a secret association called the "National Liberal Reform League," the purpose of which was to attack Christianity.[13] In December, 1869, the League determined to publish a paper, of which Ward was to be editor and principal contributor. The first issue of *The Iconoclast* appeared on March 15, 1870, and the paper managed to survive for eighteen monthly issues.[14] It was a sorry, four-page affair, with much of the material lifted from other sources. Ward's chief theme was the necessity of mental and religious liberty in an age of rational progress. The Church with its irrational dogmas opposed science as error opposes truth, and specifically Ward could point to the current movement to include Christianity in the Federal Constitution, and to clerical opposition to the spread of scientific instruction in the schools and colleges.[15] In the first number, the editor disavowed the intention of advocating any particular religious or secular theories, but within a few months he was endorsing Comtean positivism with its utilitarian and humanitarian emphases as the creed of all enlightened men.[16]

11. Spencer to Savage, *The Christian Register*, March 29, 1883, quoted in part in E. F. A. Goblet d'Alviella, *The Contemporary Evolution of Religious Thought in England, America, and India,* translated by J. Moden (New York, 1886), p. 220.

12. B. J. Stern, ed., *Young Ward's Diary* (New York, 1935), pp. 286–287.

13. *Ward's Diary,* pp. 304, 308.

14. L. F. Ward, *Glimpses of the Cosmos* (6 vols., New York, 1913), I, 42–43.

15. *The Iconoclast,* I, no. 1 (March, 1870). Reprinted in Ward, *Glimpses of the Cosmos,* I, 44–46.

16. *The Iconoclast,* I, no. 8 (Nov., 1870). Reprinted in Ward, *Glimpses of the Cosmos,* I, 99–101.

But for the distinction later achieved by its editor *The Icono-clast* merits no more attention than any of the other anti-religious periodicals which sprang up in the period and flourished for a brief day. Abner Kneeland's old Boston *Investigator* continued on under Horace Seaver and J. P. Mendum to urge completely secular thinking. It was joined in the post-war era by a host of similar journals. H. L. Green, later prominent in Abbot's National Liberal League, published the *Free Thought Magazine* in Chicago. At San Francisco appeared *The Pacific Liberal*, "devoted to Free Thought, Radical Reform, and the Secularization of the State." The editor declared himself to be a "hylotheist," and predicted that bloody conflict would shortly exterminate Christianity. D. M. Bennett, the editor of *The Truth Seeker*, attacked the Christian denial of intellectual liberty under cover of ecclesiastical supervision of public morals; he was soon to find himself imprisoned for immoral use of the mails under the Comstock law. An ambitious young promoter named Asa K. Butts saw the financial possibilities of the movement. After ruining Abbot's promising *Index* in 1872 by overestimating its immediate capacity for circulation Butts established a publishing house in New York for the printing of radical religious and secular tracts. Butts' magazine *Evolution* (1877–1880) featured articles on science and religion by the free religious leaders. Periodical readers of the 'sixties and 'seventies might also have chanced upon copies of *The Commoner, The New Age, The Friend of Progress, The Modern Thinker, The Agnostic,* or *The Freethinkers' Magazine.*[17] Few of these magazines survived for a decade or reached a maximum circulation of a thousand copies an issue, but the mere list of titles suggests something of the flavor of the Religion of Humanity as a popular crusade.

Another group in some respects related to the militant freethinkers was the Spiritualists. Earlier in the century Spiritualism appeared in the less sophisticated Christian sects, but persistent opposition among the orthodox had driven it into the anti-Christian group by 1865. The Civil War made Spiritualism a religious phenomenon of the first importance. The pretension of its mediums to prove the reality of the spiritual world by scientific methods gave a pseudo-rationalistic flavor to a faith having little

17. Most of these journals were too ephemeral to receive mention even in F. L. Mott, *A History of American Magazines* (3 vols., Cambridge, Mass., 1930–1938), III, 88–89.

else of a positive character in common with rationalism. It was this aspect of Spiritualism which presumably attracted the interest of Lester F. Ward, who frequently attended seances and seems for a time, at least, to have been a disciple of Robert Dale Owen.[18] Although Ward soon lost his faith in spirit rappings, so many Americans retained theirs that as late as 1870 Ward predicted that Spiritualism would one day become the prevailing faith of America.[19]

In inviting the Spiritualists to share the work of the Free Religious Association the radical theists saw the wider significance of the movement as a manifestation of a vital religious spirit. Spiritualism was considered to be an indication of the craving of the popular mind for the supernatural. Spiritual agencies were believed to be at work constantly, binding this world to the hereafter, and breaking down the barriers between the two worlds erected by the traditional religions. Free religion saw in Spiritualism another promise of the realization of heaven on earth, the millennium. Spiritualists denied the orthodox teaching that this world and the next were separated by an impassable gulf. They denied that the character of life after death was in any way contingent upon this life, since progress was the law of the spiritual as well as of the physical world. Orthodox dogmas concerning probation, retribution, heaven and hell, and depravity were swept away, along with the need for a Christ, an atoning sacrifice, sacraments, or priesthood.[20]

The negative aspect of Spiritualism as a criticism of orthodox concepts naturally interested the radical intellectuals more than its naive affirmations. A later generation, however, can detect a profound agreement uniting both parties in a great American religious tradition: each shared the millennial hope.[21] For the Spiritualists it was a simple assurance based upon information received in spirit communications. The rationalistic theists were too sophisticated to share such crude ideas, but their faith in a humanistic millennium on earth found universal expression as a sort of perfectionism replacing the heavenly goal of traditional

18. *Ward's Diary*, pp. 281, 282, 283, 287, 307.

19. *The Iconoclast*, I, no. 8 (Nov., 1870), *Glimpses of the Cosmos*, I, 96–98.

20. O. B. Frothingham, "The Drift Period in Theology," *The Christian Examiner*, 5 ser., XVII (July, 1865), 12–15.

21. The significance of millennialism in mid-nineteenth century religious thought is indicated in R. H. Gabriel, *The Course of American Democratic Thought*, pp. 34–36.

religion. D. A. Wasson declared the dream of perfection to be the most essential characteristic of man's nature. It reflected all of his distinctive genius, and inspired his highest performances. "It hovers before him as an ideal, and makes the impulse, the guidance, and the goal of progress." [22] Rabbi Isaac M. Wise spoke for the more rationalistic wing when he agreed that reason could lead man to perfection.[23] Again, the very kernel of free religion for Francis Abbot was its faith in man as a Progressive Being. In spite of the disappointments of the present, man retained his spiritual vision of society as it ought to be, and it was this faith which made the new creed a religion.[24] Such illustrations might be piled up without number. Millennialism of this type was closely related to the social utopianism of the time, and Abbot stated no more than the truth when he declared it to be the goal of aspiration, replacing the Kingdom of Heaven.[25]

The symbolic word that the humanist revolt set over against Christianity was Science. The Cult of Science formed rapidly after 1865. It found its devil in the irrational dogmas of traditional religion; its demigods in the great scientists, especially Darwin; its popularizers in Draper, E. L. Youmans, and Bob Ingersoll. It had its popular magazines of science, its Herbert Spencer Clubs, and its powerful publishing house—the Appleton Scientific Series. Each new advance in scientific knowledge was looked upon as revealing another segment of reality about which the superstition born of mystery could no longer cling.[26] Because the aim of science was simply to know the truth, said Lester Frank Ward, it has elevated, enlightened, and made happy mankind. Theology, on the other hand, had brought few if any beneficial results.[27] To prove the earnestness of his conviction Ward proceeded to devote the rest of his life to scientific and sociological studies.

There is no doubt but that the anti-religious animus of the rationalists was due in part, at least, to the firm stand of orthodox Christianity upon an uncompromising formulation of ancient

22. F. R. A., *Freedom and Fellowship in Religion,* pp. 370–372.

23. F. R. A., *Freedom and Fellowship in Religion,* p. 380.

24. F. E. Abbot, "What is Free Religion?" *The Index,* I (Jan. 15, 1870), 2–3.

25. For a discussion of the relation of free religion to social reform see Chapter VII.

26. F. R. A., *Proceedings, 1871,* pp. 72–73.

27. *The Iconoclast,* I, no. 2 (April, 1870). Reprinted in Ward, *Glimpses of the Cosmos,* I, 53–55.

dogmas. But on the other hand, more important than any opposition to new scientific theories was the opposition of Christianity to the humanist spirit underlying the whole movement.
The historian cannot do justice to the spirit of the Christian opposition to the new science unless he recognizes the anti-Christian moral and religious overtones accompanying the deification
of science by the rationalists.[28] The persuasive power of the Religion of Humanity was most clearly demonstrated in the complete-
ness with which it absorbed the new science, in itself neutral as
far as moral or ethical values were concerned, into an optimistic
cosmology where science was made to provide seemingly conclusive evidence of progressive mundane existence. Inherent in the
natural order of things were all the values to which man in his
highest moments aspired.

The new humanism found its immediate intellectual source in
Emersonian transcendentalism, which explained the great personal prestige of the Concord seer in the post-war era when transcendentalism had practically ceased to exert influence as a system
of thought. Material prosperity and the rapid development of
the country, rationalized in the doctrine of progress, lent humanism the apparent sanction of the natural processes. The
culmination of a successful humanitarian crusade in the abolition
of slavery indicated its capacity to achieve results. The humanitarian movements of the pre-war era had been spectacular because of their novelty, but, paradoxically, it seems safe to
conclude that humanitarianism did not entrench itself firmly in
the American character until the Gilded Age. Humanitarian humanism colored many if not all of the most distinctive types of
social and religious thought in the later nineteenth century. The
Reverend Rowland Connor declared it to be the real religion of
America. "We will not ask," he told the Free Religious Association, "where did a man come from; or, where will he go to; but,
what shall he do while he is here in this world. . . . We will stop
looking upward to the clouds for the throne of God; we will seek
instead for how much of divinity we can find in man." [29] But

28. See B. J. Loewenberg, "The Controversy over Evolution in New England,"
*The New England Quarterly,* VIII (June, 1935), 232–257. By overlooking the fact
that the new science was appropriated by atheists and radical theists in support
of their campaign against Christianity Mr. Loewenberg was able to confine attention to the intellectual phase of the controversy, putting the case against the
orthodox Christians in the worst possible light. For them, however, the issue was
primarily a religious one, on which we hesitate to pass so sweeping a judgment.

29. F. R. A., *Proceedings, 1869,* p. 98.

devotion to humanity, he added, was only the practical embodiment of religion. Standing on the platform of humanitarianism he reached out his hands toward the Infinite, and this constituted his religion. Such recourse to the Infinite as the source of its practical endeavor and the guarantor of its humanist values was the distinctive position of free religion within the humanist movement.

Free religion was the theistic crust of late nineteenth century humanism. However, to oppose the dogmas of Christianity and yet retain a vague theism reflected formalized intellectual necessities not shared by the majority of those comprising the Religion of Humanity. They were practical humanitarians concerned with mankind's immediate problems. Walt Whitman expressed their view in his projected lecture on religion.[30] Each religion, he declared, voicing a widely held nineteenth century opinion, was true in its time and place. Christianity was the truest of all, but it too was fixed to its time, and, by implication, was now to be superseded. Whitman turned to a religion of humanity, emphasizing with Emerson the divinity of man. He did not deny God so much as disavow all interest in Him. On the problem of deity his ideas were consequently hazy in the extreme. His close friend was Bob Ingersoll, whose crude sallies at the expense of the Orthodox delighted the old man of Camden immensely.[31] Yet he did not forget his early indebtedness to transcendentalism, expressing much interest in the "secondary transcendental group" (Weiss, Johnson, and Frothingham) when the faithful Traubel informed him of their work. Whitman professed not to have read them because of his distaste for controversial theology. Significantly, they were among the pronounced theists of the free religious group. Felix Adler was another of Whitman's valued friends, and the nineteenth century offered no finer example of the agnostic type than the founder of Ethical Culture. Yet, if Traubel reported him accurately, the poet declared that "ethical fellows . . . lacked the uplook." [32] The contradictions revealed in these personal loyalties reflected the confusion of his thinking. Whitman's preoccupation with humanity and indifference to theistic problems typified a large segment of the liberal thought of the day.

Although it should be apparent that the character of the cult

30. C. J. Furness, ed., *Walt Whitman's Workshop* (Cambridge, Mass., 1928), pp. 43–44.

31. Horace Traubel, *With Walt Whitman in Camden* (3 vols., Boston, 1906), I, 126 and passim.

32. Traubel, *Whitman*, I, 125–126.

of science was determined by the optimistic and humanistic presuppositions which underlay it rather than by any inherent values
in the new scientific discoveries,[33] it cannot be denied that in certain instances scientific developments exerted strong influence
upon changing modes of thought. One of the chief examples is
found in the passing of transcendentalism, which proved too
mystical, in its New England form, to survive in a naturalistic
age.[34] The new naturalism which rode in upon the influx of
evolutionary ideas after 1859 employed an empirical and historical approach to phenomena, as opposed to the immediate intuitive perception of the meaning of experience stressed by transcendentalism. According to the evolutionary teaching, intellectual
and moral qualities were accumulations of inherited racial experience, in contrast to that of transcendentalism, which placed
its faith in the original, intuitive faculties of the mind.[35] The
new philosophy was sometimes called "neo-sensationalism," or
"the philosophy of experience," by contemporaries,[36] because it
explained *a priori* ideas on the basis of hereditary transmission of
accumulated experience. Popular or semi-philosophical thought
had come full cycle when the sensationalism in its Lockean-Uni-
tarian form rejected by transcendentalism returned to constitute
the basis of the neo-rationalism which now in turn undermined
transcendentalism.

Nevertheless, of all the religious groups in America before the
Civil War, only one had expressed a cordial sympathy for the
methods and results of the new science—the transcendentalists.
The explanation of this paradox seems to lie in the relatively
neglected naturalistic aspect of transcendentalism. We are frequently told of Emerson's lack of interest in science because of
its atomistic presuppositions, and we forget that atomism was but
one of several scientific traditions in the nineteenth century. The
title of Emerson's most representative essay was, significantly,
*Nature;* and prefaced to the second edition of the essay were the
familiar verses expressing the poetic forecast of the development
hypothesis:

33. A. J. Balfour points out that Darwinism, for instance, provides ammunition
indiscriminately for both theist and agnostic. *Theism and Humanism* (New York,
1915), pp. 48–50.

34. Frothingham, *Transcendentalism in New England*, p. 204.

35. C. W. Wendte, *The Wider Fellowship* (2 vols., Boston, 1927), I, 174–176.

36. Goblet d'Alviella, *Contemporary Evolution of Religious Thought*, pp. 184–
185. Frothingham, *Transcendentalism*, p. 206.

And, striving to be man, the worm
Mounts through all the spires of form.
(1849)

In fact, transcendentalism with its pantheistic religion fitted very
well the genetic tradition of scientific thought, whose most distinguished contribution was Darwinian evolution.[37] In the essay
on "Poetry and Imagination," read in 1854 to a select group in
Divinity Hall, Cambridge, without the knowledge of the college
authorities, Emerson remarked: "The electric word pronounced
by John Hunter a hundred years ago—*arrested and progressive
development*—indicating the way upward from the invisible pro-
toplasm to the highest organism—gave the poetic key to natural
science—of which the theories of Geoffroy St. Hilaire, of Oken,
of Goethe, of Agassiz, and Owen and Darwin in zoölogy and
botany, are the fruits—a hint whose power is not exhausted, showing unity and perfect order in physics." [38]

In general, the transcendentalist attitude toward Darwinism
was expressed by Moncure D. Conway, who hailed *The Origin of
Species* in 1859 as showing that Nature itself was the miracle.[39]
Transcendentalism had no literally inspired Scriptures to defend,
nor did it look upon the natural order as below the level of man,
according to the cosmological hierarchy generally prevailing
among the Protestant sects. If Mr. Darwin wished to demonstrate
that man had evolved from more primitive forms, there was all the
more cause for congratulation upon the present attainments of
the race. It was only gradually that the transcendentalists realized the implications of the historical sciences for their intuitionist
psychology, and even then not all went over to the "scientific
theism" of free religion. By emphasizing the gulf between organic
and inorganic nature Weiss and Wasson, for instance, were content to carry the transcendentalist name to the end, for until the
ineffable core of personality should be penetrated, the descriptive
analysis of reality seemed to them strictly limited in its usefulness.[40]

37. Cf. J. T. Merz, *A History of European Thought in the Nineteenth Century*
(3 vols., Edinburgh and London, 1903), II, Chapter IX.

38. *The Works of Ralph Waldo Emerson* (Riverside Edition), IV, 12. Conway,
*Autobiography*, I, 168.

39. Conway, *Autobiography*, I, 281–282.

40. J. Weiss, "Religion and Science," D. A. Wasson, "The Nature of Religion,"
both in *Freedom and Fellowship in Religion*.

The publication of *The Origin of Species* in 1859 is generally assumed to have been a focal point in American intellectual history, and is frequently designated as the event from which the new naturalistic tendencies stem.[41] In a general sense it is doubtless convenient to use a specific date to anchor a relatively intangible tendency of thought, although a more detailed examination of the period may often rob the chosen milestone of its immediate significance. This seems to be true of the year 1859. The ferment of ideas frequently works slowly, and 1859 was followed in two years by a civil conflict which effectively impeded the circulation of Darwinian ideas in America until 1865.[42] Ideas, no matter how revolutionary they may be in their implications, are impotent unless they receive widespread expression. The real conflict over Darwinism, at least in the religious world, could not open until a Darwinian party had been formed, which pushed the fight to the Orthodox and refused to allow the latest and most spectacular application of the development hypothesis to lie discreetly buried in the Reviews.[43] The Religion of Humanity, in all its phases, the Science Cult, the free religious group, and such popularizers of Darwin as Huxley, E. L. Youmans, and John Fiske, had to preach evolution for fifteen years before public attention became riveted upon the subject, and the defenders of the old Christian outlook came forth to do battle. F. H. Foster, the historian of the disintegration of Calvinism in America, has selected the year 1874 to mark the opening of the campaign against Darwinism.[44] A survey of the tremendous increase in periodical literature on the subject which came at about that time

41. B. J. Loewenberg, "The Controversy over Evolution in New England (1859–1873)," *The New England Quarterly,* VIII (June, 1935), 232–257.

42. F. H. Foster, *The Modern Movement in American Theology* (New York, 1939), pp. 38–40.

43. Loewenberg ("The Controversy over Evolution in New England, 1859–1873"), is unconvincing in his analysis of the Darwinian "controversy" in the fifteen years following the publication of *The Origin of Species.* His material from that period is drawn from the Reviews, well-established American institutions which noticed as a matter of course the current scientific publications, including those of Darwin. The fact that the Reviews usually dismissed evolution in summary fashion is no evidence of controversy, strictly speaking. Mr. Loewenberg's truly controversial material is taken without explanation from the years after 1873 with which his article does not purport to deal. At first the scientists and intellectuals accepted or rejected Darwinism as they saw fit, but it took time for the new ideas to work down and make clear their possible social and religious implications.

44. F. H. Foster, *The Modern Movement in American Theology* (New York, 1939), pp. 40–43.

substantiates his conclusion. The last phase of the conflict of religion with science had opened.

In contrast to the transcendentalist acceptance of evolution the conservative Unitarians were generally hostile. Unitarianism had boasted of its intellectual freedom from the first, but that did not compel Unitarians to accept the theories of every visionary scientist of the day. Asa Gray might receive the evolution theory enthusiastically, and even indicate for theologians a way out by accepting Darwinism as but another chapter in "the tradition of the Divine in nature." [45] But Agassiz was emphatic in his opposition, and Agassiz was an important and influential man around Boston.[46] John A. Lowell reviewed *The Origin of Species* in *The Christian Examiner* in May, 1860, dismissing the experimental work of Darwin with the comment that the author had not offered one example to prove his basic assumption that by a permanent variation one species might become in effect a different species. Lowell noted the implications for theism in Darwin's insistence upon the place of blind chance in the perfecting of the organs and instincts of beings. The reviewer chose to adhere to the theory of divine intervention in the creation of species, a theory still quite respectable among scientific men, when he concluded: "For our own part, it seems to us at once more reverent, and more consonant to the feelings implanted in our nature, to believe in an ever-acting Providence, . . . to believe that all the adaptations so admirably fitted to the need or the gratification of His creatures are the direct act of the Creator." [47] Lowell's attitude was characteristic of the vast majority of Christians. While a few of the advanced transcendental Unitarians, like Frederick H. Hedge, found no objection to evolutionary ideas because they did not touch the essentials of religion,[48] the body of Unitarians remained hostile for some years. In view of their traditional insistence upon intellectual liberty it is interesting to note that Unitarians felt obliged to attack Darwin upon scientific grounds rather than upon his contradictions of Scripture. Readers of *The Christian Examiner*, for instance, were actually treated to the unusual spectacle of a clergyman attacking a distinguished scientist

45. Foster, *The Modern Movement*, pp. 38–40.

46. B. J. Loewenberg, "The Reaction of American Scientists to Darwinism," *American Historical Review*, XXXVIII (July, 1933), 687–701.

47. *The Christian Examiner*, 5 ser., VI (May, 1860), 451, 462, 464.

48. *The Monthly Journal* of the American Unitarian Association, IV, nos. 7, 8 (July, August, 1863), 317–323.

on the ground that his conclusions were not verified by his scientific observations.[49] The evolutionary hypothesis left no room for a cosmogony based upon Scripture literalism; consequently, few orthodox believers were content to save a modified theism by accepting belief in a purely immanent deity working itself out in the universe through the evolutionary process. The establishment of this view as one of the acceptable religious positions in America was to be the work of free religion.

For the historian of ideas Darwin and the evolutionary hypothesis forge the last link in the chain of the idea of progress which stretches far back in Western history. In all probability a free religious movement based upon the popular notion of progress would have appeared without the naturalistic corroboration of Darwinism. Certainly too many factors entered into the making of free religion to allow the historian to attribute prime influence to evolution. Nevertheless, its spectacular confirmation of a developing universe, if one chose to give it that interpretation, provided valuable ammunition for free religion, especially when Darwin became anathema to the orthodox. Abbot forwarded to the naturalist a copy of his *Truths for the Times*,[50] outlining his "scientific theism," and received in reply a letter in which Darwin remarked that he "agreed with almost every word" of it.[51] The enterprising editor appears to have been successful in spreading the idea that Darwin accepted the free religious position, and, indeed, he was too honest to have done so had he not been firmly convinced that such was actually the case. *The Index*[52] of April 13, 1872, reprinted a long article from the Chicago *Tribune* recounting the spiritual pilgrimage of the great scientist to an obscure thinker in Toledo, Ohio, to find himself a religion tailored to his evolutionary theory. Actually, Darwin could scarcely be called a free religionist. In response to a plea from Abbot that he publish his religious views the naturalist replied that he was loath to do so, not having thought deeply enough on the subject.[53] Darwin does not appear to have ever reached final opinions on ultimate questions. Although he passed through a theistic phase when, sig-

49. L. J. Livermore in *The Christian Examiner*, 5 ser., XV (Nov., 1864), 339–351.
50. Index Tracts no. 1 (no date).
51. *The Index*, III (Jan. 6, 1872), 8.
52. *The Index*, III (April 13, 1872), 115.
53. Darwin to Abbot, Sept. 6, 1871. Quoted in Francis Darwin, ed., *Life and Letters of Charles Darwin* (2 vols., New York, 1887), I, 275.

nificantly, he was writing *The Origin of Species*, we have the testimony of his son that he was content at last to remain an agnostic.[54]

While the prestige of Darwin's name was being sought for Free Religion it was attached with greater impropriety to that influential social philosophy of the Gilded Age known as social Darwinism.[55] Owing more to Malthus and Herbert Spencer than to Darwin the theoretical defense of rugged individualism permeated the environment of post-Civil War America, and Free Religion had to come to terms with its teachings and spirit before perfecting the gospel of reform which Free Religion insisted was its own end product. The Darwinian view of evolution as a struggle for existence in which the fitter individuals survived through natural selection at the expense of their less favored fellows came as a god-send to economic and social individualists who carefully nourished the Malthusian and laissez-faire roots of Darwinism. Two schools of American social Darwinists vied in justifying the free competitive order. One, led by William Graham Sumner, insisted upon the importance of a hostile environment as a selective factor in eliminating the less successful. Sumner specifically repudiated the older theory of natural rights, saying that nature recognized no right save the right of the individual to make his way out of this world if he could not make his way within it. The other school avoided such harsh conclusions by attempting to fuse Jeffersonian individualism and its natural rights philosophy with the progressive implications of Darwinism. This latter view prevailed within the ranks of the Religion of Humanity.[56] There were many exceptions, however, for the opposition to Christian supernaturalism which united the group was shared by people with a wide range of social views embracing extreme individualism, moderate reformism, and socialism.

The social conflicts of industrial America were too sharp to permit such a heterogeneous group to form a permanent organization. Francis Abbot made the attempt with his National Liberal League, the rapid disintegration of which was due primarily to the inability of freethinkers to exclude social questions from an

54. Francis Darwin, *Charles Darwin,* I, 276–284.

55. Richard Hofstadter, *Social Darwinism in American Thought* (Philadelphia, 1944).

56. A characteristic encounter between Sumner and W. J. Potter, representing these two schools, is described below in Chapter VII. Each could refer with equal propriety to the authority of Darwin.

organization established to promote secularism. Within the Free Religious group itself there was no unanimity of social philosophy, although most of its members would probably have subscribed to the milder form of social Darwinism. As the full implications of radical individualism unfolded themselves in the years after Appomattox, however, and especially as their significance in the moral world became clear, Free Religion grew less cordial toward the other phases of the Religion of Humanity. It discovered that its distinguishing characteristics of theism, social conservatism, and intellectual background were in practice less important than its hold upon the traditional morality. When radical freethinkers like Ezra Heywood and Samuel P. Putnam carried their individualism in morals to the limit of defending free love, the free religionists, whose moral and spiritual values were none the less absolute for being grounded in the natural rather than in the revealed order, found themselves ranged on the side of Anthony Comstock and the outraged respectability of the day. The event in itself would have been of no importance had it not led to the sundering of the Liberal League and to the formulation by Francis Abbot of a revised or "scientific" liberalism to provide a philosophic basis for a program of reform.

The train of events that brought American secularists together for the only time in the National Liberal League had its beginning in the dark days of 1863 when Northerners everywhere were searching their souls to discover what untapped resources of loyalty and conviction remained to justify further sacrifice in a wellnigh hopeless cause. It was a time for the reassessment of fundamentals, and demand arose among certain evangelical Protestant groups of the Middle West for the establishment of the national political institutions upon an explicitly Christian foundation. Only by such a national confession of faith, it was urged, could God's displeasure be assuaged and the civil crisis averted. Representatives of eleven religious denominations met at Xenia, Ohio, on February 3, 1863 to demand the passage of a constitutional amendment that would pledge allegiance to God and submit the nation to His divine rule. A National Reform Association dominated by theologically conservative Presbyterians and Episcopalians was formed in the following year to agitate for the Christian Amendment.[57]

The sponsors of the amendment recognized that its adoption

57. *The Index,* IX (April 4, 1878), 158–159.

would constitute a major departure from the established American
political tradition. Their fundamentalist convictions were revealed
in their belief that the crisis of secession was the direct result of
God's judgment upon a nation that had deliberately turned its
back on Him, and, although predominantly Christian, had attempted to create a political state on the mere secular foundation
of natural rights and property interests. A house built upon the
sands of self-interest could scarcely expect to withstand the floods
of human passion that would periodically beat upon it. Only by
establishing within it that divine Authority to whom all men owe
allegiance could present and future crises be weathered. The new
Christian political theory as formulated by Professor Tayler
Lewis, of Union College, was frankly theocratic in nature. The
state could not be explained in purely human or rational terms.
Men might shape its forms and adjust the relations of its functions,
but its essence and ultimate powers were beyond the reach of men;
they were in fact attributes of a state religion of which God was the
head. Too many problems of the democratic state, according to
Lewis, defied solution in purely rational terms. What authority
consistent with its acknowledged principle of self-interest could be
invoked to prevent the pulverization of the Republic through
secession? What better authority than the will of the stronger
dictated the use of force to prevent secession? These nineteenth-
century theocrats ignored the elaborate exposition of Lincoln
based upon a historical conception of the development of national-
ized democratic institutions and idealism. They appealed rather to
the transcendent unity imposed upon Christians by their submission to the Lord Jesus Christ. Man could neither create nor destroy the state, which was the instrument of God's governance. The
individual's place within the state was to be conceived primarily in
terms of duties rather than of rights. The magistrates were in a
true sense ministers of God, and should be professing Christians
of high moral character. No official state church need be established. It was only necessary that there be constant devotion to the
Christian ideal, and a willingness to regard the state as a moral
being with accountability and a conscience.[58]

The theocratic movement came at a time when the wave of
evangelical Protestantism that had swept the United States in the
earlier nineteenth century was rapidly ebbing. Decades had passed
since the last established church in New England had been forced

58. *The Christian Statesman,* I (Sept. 2, 1867), 1–4, 8.

to abandon its privileges. Now for the last time a popular fundamentalist crusade was rallied by men of learning and intelligence; leaders such as Tayler Lewis, Julius Seeley of Amherst College, George Junkin of Lafayette, and Professor J. H. McIlvaine of Princeton. The Methodist Episcopal, Reformed Presbyterian, and Old School Presbyterian churches all voiced approval through their national organizations.[59] For more than ten years after Appomattox the cause was vigorously pushed. *The Christian Statesman*, organ of the movement, was widely distributed. Presbyteries in Ohio, Pennsylvania, and Illinois appropriated funds and engaged propagandists. Public meetings were held in the larger cities of the East and Middle West, while petitions to Congress demanding a Christian constitutional amendment received thousands of signatures.[60] But strong as the authority of Christianity remained in the realms of personal piety and social influence, its political prestige had been constantly waning. The true weakness of the amendment movement was revealed in the necessity it faced of advocating a state religion without a state church. It was of course impossible to establish any one of the hundreds of American sects or churches in a favored political position. Inter-denominational jealousies were only less pronounced than the fear of irreligious people and outspoken infidels. Many orthodox religious leaders joined with the secularists when the latter launched a counter-crusade to defeat the proposed amendment and reassert the traditional principles of religious liberty and the separation of church and state.

From its inception *The Index* devoted considerable attention to what Abbot conceived to be the dangers of the evangelical revival. The natural corollary of free religion was the free state, and Abbot undoubtedly exaggerated the menace of the Christian amendment to democratic traditions. The scholarship of the twentieth century which was to awaken in thoughtful Americans an appreciation of the value and significance of the Christian contri-

59. *The Index*, III (March 30, 1872), 101; IX (April 4, 1878), 158–159.
60. One form of the proposed amendment would alter the Preamble by inserting the clauses within brackets as follows: "We, the people of the United States [acknowledging Almighty God as the source of all authority and power in civil government, the Lord Jesus Christ as the Ruler among the nations, and His Will, revealed in the Holy Scriptures, as of supreme authority, in order to constitute a Christian government,] form a more perfect union, establish justice, insure domestic tranquillity, provide for the common defense, promote the general welfare, . . ." etc. *The Christian Statesman*, I (Sept. 2, 1867), 4; I (Nov. 15, 1867), 45–46. *The Index*, I (Mar. 12, 1870), 4–5.

bution to the liberal tradition was still an unexplored field. Although he himself possessed a greater awareness than many of the meaning of the Puritan tradition, Abbot nevertheless shared with many of his liberal contemporaries the conviction that Christianity and liberalism were necessarily at odds with each other. The insistence of the prevailing popular theology of the seventies upon emphasizing dogmas it was unable to endow with spiritual vitality relevant to the issues of the day largely accounted for the anti-Christian secularism of the Religion of Humanity. In 1872 Abbot sponsored the circulation of petitions to Congress against the Christian amendment. Over thirty thousand signatures were obtained in New England and the Middle West, areas where *The Index* was read.[61] Charles Sumner agreed to lead the opposition to the amendment in the Senate. When it became clear that the amendment could not command sufficient support to carry Congress the secularists went over to the offensive and under the leadership of Abbot launched a drive to sweep away the remaining vestiges of religious influence in the state.

The "Nine Demands of Liberalism" prominently displayed in *The Index* became the program around which local Liberal Leagues were organized during the 'seventies. The general purpose of the Demands was to destroy the privileges that religion still enjoyed through state favor. Ecclesiastical property should no longer be exempt from taxation. Such favors as the public appointment of chaplains, the appropriation of public funds for sectarian educational and charitable institutions, the appointment by the state of religious festivals, and the use of the Bible in the public schools, should cease. Simple affirmation should be substituted for the judicial oath. Sabbath laws and laws enforcing "Christian morality" should be repealed. No partiality should be shown to any religion in the administration of the state; all laws should conform to "the requirements of natural morality, equal rights, and impartial liberty." [62] None of these demands had any effect save perhaps the most important. Prohibitions upon sectarian instruction in public schools or upon public support of sectarian schools have subsequently been written into nearly all of the state constitutions,[63] although such reaffirmation of the traditional

61. *The Index*, III (1872), passim, especially (June 8, 1872), 180–181.
62. *The Index*, IV (Jan. 4, 1873), 1.
63. Carl Zollmann, "The Constitutional and Legal Status of Religion in Public Education," *The Journal of Religion*, II (May, 1922), 239.

secular public education should more likely be attributed to the influence of mutually jealous religious groups rather than to the efforts of secularists. Thirty-two local Leagues were formed by the end of 1875,[64] and at the Centennial Exposition in Philadelphia the following year a Congress of Liberals organized the National Liberal League.

The general purpose of the League was to achieve the complete separation of church and state. Interest in the League was at first largely confined to the free religious circle. Francis Abbot was elected president, and most of the officers were members of the Free Religious Association. Abbot, however, made a strenuous effort to attract other secularists. Among the vice-presidents were the well-known radical editors, Horace Seaver of the Boston *Investigator*, and D. M. Bennett of the *Truth Seeker*. Colonel Bob Ingersoll served on the Executive Committee.[65] Apart from the organization of the National Liberal League the only action of consequence taken by the Congress of Liberals was the adoption of a resolution introduced by B. F. Underwood favoring national and state legislation against the circulation of obscene publications and articles. The resolution cautioned, however, that these laws should be so carefully drawn as to prevent the prosecution of honest reformers and radicals who might advocate social reforms no matter how offensive to the community at large so long as the reformer observed the ordinary rules of decent utterance.[66]

The obscenity issue, thus raised at the moment of inception of the Liberal League, proved to be the rock on which organized liberalism foundered. Abbot's Demands of Liberalism had not recognized the necessity to defend the freedom of the press from bigoted religious censorship, but the left-wing secularists quickly found this principle to be involved in the activities of the post-office inspector, Anthony Comstock. Backed by Y.M.C.A. leaders and influential Protestant laymen, Comstock had persuaded Congress to pass the so-called Comstock postal laws of 1873 and 1876, prohibiting the shipment of obscene matter through the mails. The acts did not attempt to define obscenity or otherwise to provide safeguards to protect sincere critics of the prevailing sexual mores.[67] Appointed inspector, Comstock launched a spectacular

64. *The Index,* VI (Dec. 30, 1875), 614.
65. *The Index,* VII (July 13, 1876), 325–326.
66. *The Index,* IX (June 27, 1878), 307.
67. G. P. Sanger, ed., *U.S. Statutes at Large, 1871–1873* (Boston, 1873), pp. 598–600; *U.S. Statutes at Large,* XIX (Washington, 1877), 90.

drive to clean out the vendors of pornography whose large-scale operations were one of the less savory aspects of the Gilded Age.

Unfortunately, in his simple fundamentalist bigotry Comstock was unable to distinguish between obscenity and legitimate discussion of the social and moral code. Free-thinking reformers like Ezra Heywood and D. M. Bennett soon felt the weight of his hand. Heywood, a typical New England reformer who had served his apprenticeship in the liberal Unitarian, anti-slavery, and pacifist causes, turned his attention after the Civil War to reform of marriage institutions and the family. This former disciple of Theodore Parker organized the "New England Free-Love League" in 1873, the "Year of Love" on which his new system of calendar notation was based. From his own press he issued tracts on a free form of marriage unrestricted by laws and terminable at the will of either party. In his pamphlet, *Cupid's Yokes*, Heywood defended free love as a necessary consequence of private judgment in morals. Shocking though they were to Victorian sensibilities, Heywood's views were sincere enough, nor would his mode of expression have offended a twentieth-century public. He asserted that the intervention of society was not necessary to bind lovers together. The failure of many marriages he attributed to ignorance, while their continuance without love reduced the partners to bestiality. As a basis for a firmer marriage relationship he urged adequate sex knowledge, and reminded his readers that in love as in other affairs virtue was the product of liberty and conscience.[68] After two unsuccessful attempts Comstock finally secured the conviction of Heywood, who had bitterly attacked the postal inspector in his periodical, *The Word*. That the issues were religious as well as personal and moral became clear when Comstock arrested D. M. Bennett in 1877 on an obscenity charge for circulating his heretical *Open Letter to Jesus Christ*. Although the indictment was quashed, radicals realized that Comstock was fully prepared to use his powers not only to stamp out pornography and vice, but to persecute freethinkers as well. According to rumor, the vice crusader had boasted that he would close *The Word* and the *Truth Seeker* and then move upon *The Index*.

In the meantime, Abbot was attempting to guide the National Liberal League in the direction of social and political reform. At the first annual congress of the League, held in Rochester in

68. *The Index*, X (May 1, 1879), 211. Heywood Broun and Margaret Leech, *Anthony Comstock: Roundsman of the Lord* (New York, 1927), pp. 170–184.

October, 1877, he stressed the need of a "Conscience Party" in politics. Convinced that a reaction was setting in against the traditional secularist principles of political life, Abbot believed that the first plank of the new party should demand the total separation of church and state according to the principles of the Liberal League. More relevant to the dominant issues of the day was the second proposed plank, demanding national protection for national citizens. Specifically, such protection should include equal rights and suffrage for women, as well as vigorous protection of the rights of Negroes under the fourteenth and fifteenth amendments. It was already apparent by 1877 that the return of the southern states to local political control was costing the freedmen what tenuous privileges they had enjoyed under the reconstruction governments. This situation naturally aroused the reformist zeal of the liberals, many of whom formed their convictions in abolitionist days. Finally, Abbot offered his great panacea for all social ills— universal education. The third plank demanded that the states provide schools of equal efficiency for all and require each child to obtain an education adequate to equip him for the duties of citizenship in the modern world. The congress adopted Abbot's platform, and D. M. Bennett urged the immediate formation of the Conscience Party, with Col. Bob Ingersoll and Abbot as presidential and vice-presidential candidates, respectively. Ingersoll was not present, and presumably had not been consulted, while Abbot refused to consider political candidacy. Majority sentiment furthermore counseled the postponement of political action until the League should have time to increase its strength. The question of entering the campaign of 1880 was consequently deferred to the League congress of the following year.

Before the Congress of Liberals convened again, however, the arrest of D. M. Bennett in November, 1877, for circulating "obscene and blasphemous" publications, raised in acute form the issue of free speech and pushed the question of politics into the background. Bennett's offense consisted in mailing copies of his *Open Letter to Jesus Christ* and a scientific treatise dealing with propagation among marsupials. Failing to silence Bennett, Comstock turned upon Heywood and finally secured the latter's arrest and conviction a few months later. Although it was apparent enough that Comstock was attempting to use his official powers to suppress religious infidelity, and that organized liberalism should unite to resist the encroachment upon its rights of free speech in religious matters, the issue only divided the liberals into two factions which became increasingly hostile to one another.

One faction under the leadership of D. M. Bennett, with the *Truth Seeker* as its spokesman, demanded the immediate repeal of all obscenity legislation as being in violation of the constitutional right of individuals to hold any social, moral, or political opinions they wished. Mental and moral health, they believed, could better be secured by virtue and knowledge than by ignorance and coercion. As extreme individualists they resented the restraints society imposes upon its members, and they believed it to be axiomatic with all true reform that the liberty gained necessarily involves a certain amount of license.[69] These views were embodied in a petition to Congress circulated by friends of the *Truth Seeker* demanding the immediate repeal of the Comstock laws. These radical individualists were not always true to their principles, however. As Abbot was quick to point out, upon occasion they would concede the right of states if not the federal government to regulate and punish obscenity.[70] Heywood, it was true, adhered consistently to his position of philosophical anarchism, and Benjamin R. Tucker, who edited *The Word* for him while the free-love apologist languished in Dedham jail, complained of the tendency of Bennett and his followers to desert their free-love brethren in the face of the journalistic furor that naturally resulted.[71]

Abbot warned his *Index* constituency of the dire consequences for organized liberalism should it follow the lead of the Bennett group. The issue was not simply one of freedom of speech and press, as Bennett maintained; it involved the definition of the limits of free speech short of obscenity. The moral sense of the liberal theists was shocked by the tendency of the more extreme radicals to dabble with theories of free love. They also maintained that it was right and necessary for the federal government to suppress obscenity by legislation so carefully phrased as to permit serious discussion of any subject, even free love. This was the position officially adopted by the National Liberal League in 1876. They agreed with the radicals that prosecutions for blasphemy represented precisely the kind of church-state relationship the Liberal League was pledged to destroy, but they insisted that free

69. *The Index*, VIII (Dec. 20, 1877), 606–607; IX (Jan. 31, 1878), 56–57.
70. *The Index*, IX (Jan. 31, 1878), 55; (Sept. 26, 1878), 462–463.
71. *The Index*, IX (Dec. 12, 1878), 589.

speech and press were no defense for breaches of the established canons of propriety. This position was dictated by considerations more significant than mere Victorian delicacy. If liberalism were to enter the political realm, due regard must be paid to the almost universal tendency of the orthodox community to identify religious infidelity with immorality. Abbot believed it would be political suicide not to make it perfectly clear that liberals despised and hated obscenity and were fully prepared to use police powers to suppress it. By defining as obscene any utterance the main intent of which was to pander to the passions of the young or puerile, he thought that the law would be effective for its purpose yet unavailable to bigots like Comstock who would suppress legitimate publications addressed to the thinking faculties. In Abbot's opinion, *Cupid's Yokes* clearly belonged in this latter class, for although the views expressed were to him offensive and pernicious he considered it the height of folly to class them as obscene.[72]

To the protest of Bennett and his individualist followers that government had no business to interfere in matters of private conduct [73] Abbot was able to point to the recent action of the Supreme Court in sustaining the constitutionality of the obscenity laws. No further discussion appeared to be necessary. It was important, however, to allay the fears of liberals generally that once the right of the state to interfere in matters of morals was admitted, nothing could prevent government from intervening to suppress irreligious publications as well, because of the prevailing tendency to identify immorality with irreligion. Abbot's discussion of the rôle of democratic government in a free society was designed to clarify this issue. He represented human activity in terms of three concentric circles, the innermost symbolizing the proper sphere of government action. All government, he believed, had its origin in the conflict of human wills and passions in society. Democratic government presumed to settle these conflicts through the expressed will of the majority. It also assumed that every man was free to do as he pleased so long as he did not violate the equal

72. *The Index,* VIII (Dec. 6, 1877), 582–583.

73. T. B. Wakeman, a member of the New York bar, had defended Heywood and Bennett on the ground that the Comstock laws were an unconstitutional violation of free speech and press. *The Index,* IX (Sept. 26, 1878), 462–463. Aside from Wakeman's argument, however, the power of Congress under the Constitution to exclude obscene matter from the mails has never seriously been questioned. Lindsay Rogers, *The Postal Power of Congress. A Study in Constitutional Expansion* (Baltimore, 1916), pp. 48–49, 51 and note.

rights of his fellows, and it defined a crime as a gross violation of these equal rights. Thus it might be said that government dealt with human conduct in its abnormal rather than in its normal aspects. This was the carefully circumscribed sphere of governmental action in nineteenth-century democratic society. A larger circle, embracing the governmental sphere as well as much that was outside of it, designated what Abbot considered the proper province of morality. Certain immoral acts, such as murder, arson, or adultery, were clearly also crimes, and as such were subject to penalties inflicted by the state. But since all human conduct was germaine to moral considerations many moral issues must arise over which the state would have no control. Heywood's free-love theories belonged in this category. It was Abbot's contention that the obscenity laws should be so carefully drawn as to prevent zealous or bigoted governmental agents from exceeding the limits of authority already defined in general by the popular will. The third and outermost circle represented the sphere of religion, embracing the others, but subject to them only insofar as religious views might impinge upon morality or civil affairs. In other words, although the state might conceivably interfere in religious affairs should the views or practices in question be criminal in character, religion as generally professed was almost entirely beyond the province of state concern. By means of this diagrammatic representation Abbot attempted to show that great as was the distinction between the obscene and the immoral, that between the obscene and the irreligious was infinitely greater.[74]

In his zeal to prevent the liberal movement from becoming identified with the defense of obscenity and free love Abbot made it more difficult to effect with the opposing faction a compromise that might have held the Liberal League together. He advised his readers not to sign the petition sponsored by the *Truth Seeker* requesting Congress to repeal the Comstock laws. In the summer of 1878 the House Committee on Revision of the Laws refused to consider any modification of the existing postal laws.[75] When he was bitterly attacked by Bennett as a traitor to the liberal movement Abbot retaliated with the assertion that Bennett had attached to his petition, without authorization, the name of McKesson and Robbins, wholesale druggists, citing an item in the New York

74. *The Index*, IX (Oct. 10, 1878), 486.
75. *The Index*, IX (June 13, 1878), 282–283.

*Tribune* stating that the druggists were bringing suit against Bennett. Before the journalistic skirmish ended each faction had conceived a violent enmity for the other, and each was determined to impose its views upon the League at the annual congress of 1878. In vain did Col. Bob Ingersoll hold aloof from the controversy and attempt to reconcile the "repealers" and the "reformers." The drive for increased League membership became a factional struggle for power.[76]

For the second time in his career Abbot was to taste defeat at Syracuse. When the second annual congress assembled there in October it was apparent that a majority of the 138 delegates were "repealers," although the committees chosen by the congress proved to be under the control of the "reformers." Abbot and his fellow officers had announced publicly that they would accept office again only on condition that the League approve in principle the right of states and federal government to suppress obscenity.[77] No sooner had the congress assembled than the majority took control of the proceedings from the officers and committees and with much wrangling and disorder attempted to have its own way. Abbot and Judge E. P. Hurlbut offered resolutions on behalf of the "reformers" defending freedom of the press for serious discussion of moral questions, even though occasional indecencies might appear. They demanded, however, such modifications of the Comstock laws as would restrict Comstock's activities to the suppression of obvious pornography. Since the majority did not care to assume the rôle of defenders of pornography, although they were determined to defeat Abbot, they passed a motion by Courtlandt Palmer to defer the question to the congress of the following year. Abbot observed that this action left the matter where it had been since 1876, when the League had committed itself to reform.[78]

Thus temporarily out-maneuvered the majority cried for the blood of the officers. The recommendation of the nominating committee that Abbot and his fellow officers be reëlected was set aside, and a new slate of officers headed by Elizur Wright was elected with acclamation. The founder of the Liberal League was repudiated by his own organization. Since all of the newly elected officers were known to favor outright repeal of the Comstock laws Abbot

76. *The Index,* IX (1878), 30, 56, 234–235, 258–259, 332.
77. *The Index,* IX (Sept. 19, 1878), 450.
78. *The Index,* IX (Nov. 7, 1878), 534–536.

and his party considered their election a violation of the earlier agreement to postpone consideration of the obscenity question for another year. At the suggestion of Judge Hurlbut the reformers withdrew from the League and formed a new organization of their own, the National Liberal League of America.[79] Neither league survived the schism for long. The deep disparities in temper which were at bottom the cause of the division made it clear that the liberal spirit must work out its destiny as a leaven in many parties and movements, without a home of its own.

The brief history of the Liberal League culminating in the conflict with the extreme individualists led Francis Abbot to develop more fully his philosophy of "reformed" liberalism. The riotous sessions at Syracuse convinced him of the bankruptcy of anarchistic individualism and drove him to search for a naturalistic or scientific basis for a social order. A line of thought was already at hand in the free religious conception of faith substantiated empirically by universal human experience. Abbot believed that a comparable criterion for the establishment of social values was to be found in his conception of "the consensus of the competent," or the authority of universal reason based upon the social experience of mankind.[80]

A second event confirmed Abbot's conviction that unrestrained individualism would lead directly to moral chaos. A member of the Free Religious Association, the Reverend Samuel P. Putnam, Unitarian minister at Northfield, Massachusetts, had written occasionally to the *Index* editor during 1877 to express his dissatisfaction with Abbot's scientific theism as a basis for religious faith.[81] Putnam professed to be a disciple of the transcendentalists. Finding his religious inspiration to be inner and unique, he refused to submit to criteria derived from universal religious experience. He was prepared to accept the teaching of science on material matters, but until science could either prove or disprove his inner beliefs he proposed to follow the promptings of his impulses, since they gave him great joy and power. What had science to say of the moral sentiments, which welled up spontaneously out of human

79. *The Index,* IX (Nov. 7, 1878), 536–537. Comstock's inimitable account of the Liberal League, omitting none of the unsavory details, may be found in his *Frauds Exposed; or, How the People are Deceived and Robbed, and Youth Corrupted* (New York, 1880), pp. 388–515.

80. *The Index,* X (March 13, 1879), 126–127.

81. *The Index,* VIII (May 17, 1877), 234–236; (July 26, 1877), 354–356; (Nov. 15, 1877), 546–548.

nature? What proof supplied by the intellect could compare in vividness with the instinct that tells us ingratitude is wrong? Putnam was particularly anxious to insist that moral feelings were none the less real for being entirely subjective. The rôle of radicalism was to prepare the way for a society in which external restraints would be swept away in order that men would be free to follow their own best impulses.

Abbot summoned what patience he could to demolish this travesty upon moral freedom. Truth in any field, whether of science or morals, rested, he replied, upon universal reason. Scientific truth is arrived at through prolonged experiment and discussion, until the consensus of competent people is agreed upon the principle in question. Similarly, moral axioms are originally intellectual propositions ultimately confirmed and ground into human nature by the process of socio-moral growth. This was the opinion shared by Samuel Butler and other evolutionists of the time. It was still possible for nineteenth-century thinkers to believe as Abbot did that a survey of history demonstrated the gradual perfection of moral and social institutions through the accumulated experience of the race. This experience, however, only revealed the truth of the age-old law of moral reciprocity, found at least as early as Confucius, who said in anticipation of the Golden Rule, "What you do not want done to yourself, do not do to others." The process of history was not, then, that of uncovering new secrets but of approximating old truths. In the search for the good life, reason must precede and clarify sentiment. The mixture of rationalist and evolutionary thinking revealed here was characteristic of Abbot's transitional position.

The practical consequence, as well as possible cause, of the Rev. Mr. Putnam's inquiries was revealed by announcements in the press, in the spring of 1879, that he had deserted his wife for another woman. He defended his course in the *Truth Seeker*, that champion of radical individualism, with arguments similar to those already mentioned. The necessity to follow the dictates of his conscience, "the gift of heaven," seemed to be his only alternative to "Rome." [82] Abbot's argument, however, had impressed him to the extent that he appealed from the average moral sentiment of his day to the "enlightened judgment of the future," convinced that the restraints of the present marriage system would

82. *The Index*, X (March 27, 1879), 150–151.

then be judged as degrading the most delicate affections. Thus a prominent member of the Free Religious Association espoused the free-love principles of Ezra Heywood.[83]

These events had a profound effect upon Abbot and a majority of the free religionists. They raised an insuperable barrier between the Association and the main body of the Religion of Humanity. Thenceforth Free Religion recognized a closer kinship with the religious than with the secular tradition, and ultimately its younger adherents found their way back into the Unitarian and other liberal Christian churches.

Abbot was now convinced that liberalism needed reform as badly as Christianity. The former radical Republican declared in 1879 that the liberal individualism of the nineteenth century, once the enemy of tyranny, had run its course, and that it now obstructed necessary change. The tendency of the age was towards unity in politics and universality in thought. The growth of cities, the consolidation of nationalities, and the development of international services all seemed to indicate a closer integration of humanity. Similarly, the spectacular advances of theoretical and applied science demonstrated the universality of natural law. The arbitrary will and moral irresponsibility of extreme individualism could find no place in such a world, and the sooner it was replaced by a social philosophy recognizing the corporate obligations of the individual the better.[84] The new liberalism must show the individual's conscience to be a factor in the corporate conscience of the community. It must teach men that they are morally responsible for the public acts of the corporations to which they belong. Finally, it should insist upon the authority of universal reason expressed in the consensus of the competent as the arbiter between conflicting men of good will in all the affairs of life.[85]

Abbot's principle of the consensus of the competent received a good deal of criticism from his contemporaries. In the process of defining it more closely he clarified his own position with respect to older and later thought currents. W. D. LeSueur observed that truth frequently resided with the minority or even with one. If in such cases there were no appeal from the reigning consensus of opinion progress would be stultified.[86] Abbot con-

83. *The Index,* X (April 24, 1879), 201.
84. *The Index,* X (March 20, 1879), 138–139.
85. *The Index,* X (March 13, 1879), 126–127.
86. *The Index,* X (April 17, 1879), 187.

ceded that the authority of private judgment was of equal weight with that of the consensus of the day, but only because both deferred to the ultimate judgment of fact and logical argument. This final verdict would be delivered and sustained by a truly competent consensus. It might brand the individual judgment as saintly, criminal, or foolish. Every science possesses a large body of truths thus established, along with more tentatively held theories and hypotheses. The achievements of science rest upon reverence for fact as interpreted by universal reason.

A parallel situation pertained in the moral realm, although here Abbot's argument was less convincing. Society embodies its moral judgments in laws which, if public opinion has been properly canvassed, are an approximation to the consensus of opinion of the intelligent citizenry. Since for practical reasons lawmaking cannot await unanimous consent, laws are seen to be partly real and partly conventional. Abbot's identification of moral imperatives with the expressed will of the majority, fundamental though it is in the democratic ideology, must have rung strangely in contemporary ears, when men were concerned chiefly to protect the economic interests of the individual from regulation by society.

Furthermore, his rationalistic presuppositions, evident throughout the discussion, led to a certain oversimplification of the historical process that detracted from the fruitfulness of his analysis. Convinced that the highly interdependent character of modern civilization together with the increase in literacy were constantly swelling the ranks of the competent in all fields, he assumed that it was no longer possible for any man to be greatly in advance of the age, although he bitterly conceded that many might lag behind it. But the very factors assumed to promote the consolidation of society might very well help to disrupt it. The consensus of competent biologists in Abbot's day might be in agreement as to the adequacy of Darwin's explanation of evolution through variation and natural selection. This did not mean that they would still agree twenty years later. Nor did agreement upon the Darwinian hypothesis help to assimilate its implications in other fields of thought. In an age of profound readjustment there was but cold comfort in an appeal to the bar of the competent. Nevertheless, Abbot's faith in universal reason interpreted by the competent revealed his monistic and rationalistic presuppositions. In social affairs this rationalism sustained an innate conservatism that provided no place for actual experimentation. Although he associated with C. S. Peirce and William James there was no hint in his thought of the new pragmatism that was to judge an idea not by its fate at the theoretical bar of the competent but by its success in practice.

# HUMANITARIAN RELIGION—A FAITH FOR REFORM

THE distinctive thought of late nineteenth-century America was humanistic in character, inspired largely by the European rationalism of the previous two centuries. Complacent in the spectacular achievements of his democratic political system the American thinker absorbed the new historical consciousness that was developing so rapidly, confident that it would only confirm and strengthen his understanding and control of his destiny. The humanistic outlook with its emphasis on man as the central and creative factor in the drama of life, wedded to the sharpened sense of his place in history, largely governed prevailing attitudes toward the new historical sciences of geology and evolutionary biology. The mechanistic and amoral implications of Darwinism were largely disregarded in favor of an interpretation that confirmed the blandest assumptions of human progress. Finally, the rise of sociology as a discipline with scientific pretensions was a direct product of the new humanism in that it displayed a primary interest in human affairs for their own sake rather than as subsidiary or incidental to other considerations.

It has already been seen how such a reorientation of interest produced a new attitude toward religion. In increasing numbers men began to see their faith as the product of social experience. Whether the religion thus generated took the form of Christianity, non-Christian theism, positivism, or agnosticism was of minor importance. The common method of derivation was the new element of significance. The great sociological systems of the nineteenth century, those of Spencer, Comte, Ward, and Morgan, used this approach in their treatment of religious problems. When Frothingham remarked that "the interior spirit of any age is the spirit of God; and no faith can be living that has that spirit against it; no Church can be strong except in that alliance," [1] he was expressing the free religious version of the same

1. Frothingham, *The Religion of Humanity*, p. 7.

idea. Abbot put it more bluntly when he declared that the root of religion is universal human nature.

The nineteenth-century rationalist who considered the doctrine of evolution the crowning jewel in the diadem of human intelligence, who saw the old religious faith reeling under the blows of biblical criticism, and the rise of new humanistic systems which ignored the old absolutes—such a person was compelled to make radical readjustments in his outlook if he were to save the essentials of his religious faith. Obviously, the vividness of the traditional Christian relationship between man and his God was irretrievably lost. The new creed, according to Frothingham, must start from new premises and come to new conclusions.

To begin with, it throws God into a cloudy background where the individual cannot hope to reach Him with complaint or petition, and so completely merges providence in law that care for individual needs cannot be thought of. Special interpositions for the help of mankind are inconceivable, and special revelations for the instruction of mankind are out of place. Man begins at a low beginning and slowly makes his way upward by progressive steps, instead of being on a high level of spiritual attainment, and being sustained there by divine assistance. The Christ is a development from the stock of humanity, no superhuman personage sent to redeem the race; no miracles attest a power above nature; no communication of heavenly life avouches a Son of God. The bible, old testament and new, falls into the category of human literature. The tide of history rolls over the place where the Saviour listened for heavenly voices, and watched at night with his disciples. The legends of apostolic inspiration are discredited. In the vast reaches of time required to develop mankind, nations live but a comparative moment. Epochs are no more than instants and may scarcely make a ripple on the surface of the flood of time. Forms of life may themselves vanish; species disappear. The waves of being swell and subside; races emerge to be again submerged beneath the wave; civilizations flash like foam—bubbles in the sun that gleam and burst, the sorrows and joys, the virtues and vices of millions leaving no visible trace on the surface of the great deep.[2]

Perhaps to compensate for the loss of sympathy and strength derived from personal contact with the divine Being, the feeling

2. Frothingham, *Creed and Conduct*, pp. 12–14.

of the brotherhood of man acquired a new importance. The activist traditions in American life tended to identify humanitarianism with social reform. Typical humanitarianism did not appear as mere concern for the unfortunate, expressed in charity or almsgiving. It struck at the root of evils in society, as found in faulty institutions; and it proposed to set up new ones. The American democratic faith assumed that man was good, although he might be hampered in his normal development by specific social evils. Since the age put its faith in the values and capacities of the individual it tended to seek its evils in institutions, impersonal agencies which restricted the freedom of the individual. Throughout the nineteenth century one institution or another was the object of prime suspicion, first the state, then slavery, finally the corporation, to mention only the more important. Wendell Phillips, a prominent figure at the early meetings of the Free Religious Association, illustrated another aspect of the same attitude when he remarked that the reason why the religion of the day was "in a corrupt and hide-bound and marvelously decrepit state is because society, which forms its body here, is a capital-punishment, pro-slavery, fourteen-hours-a-day, woman-under-the-heel society; and as long as it is, the soul that dwells in that body must be a soul dwelling in darkness." [3] If man produced his own religion it was obvious that the defects of his environment would be reflected in it.

As one of the most vigorous expressions of spiritual individualism in the post-Civil War era free religion reserved its chief scorn for the churches. They were inert institutions, bound to the social order with all its defects, coercing the individual by their asserted monopoly over the attainment of salvation. Wendell Phillips had started life with the conviction that the church was the reservoir of the best religious feeling, and he had been "bayoneted out of this conviction" by the realization that the churches were irrevocably opposed to any reform movement. He was forced to conclude that an organization was unable by its very nature to accept a new idea. [4] The struggle within the Association over the question of organized activity could only be understood when it was seen to involve a deep conviction among many members of the dire effects of organization upon the life of the spirit. Pure religion, according to Ednah D. Cheney, was the animating spirit of

3. F. R. A., *Procedings, 1868,* p. 95.
4. *Freedom and Fellowship in Religion,* pp. 413–416.

one's whole life, but when it became solidified in organized ecclesiasticism nothing was more obstinate and bitter in its resistance to necessary change. The superiority of free religion in its relation to social reform, she believed, lay in its native freedom, untrammeled by tradition or creed, and uncommitted to any social institutions. Most of all, it had the requisite faith in humanity.[5] The humanitarian enthusiasm for tinkering with the social order was based upon the assumption that the individual was competent to assess its evils and prescribe the remedy. Freedom was necessary to practice such a philosophy, and free religion extended to the reformer the prime essential, a philosophy of freedom from external bonds through subjection to the inner law. On these grounds Frothingham was convinced that free religion was inevitably the philosophy of all social reformers.[6]

The optimism of the post-Civil War era was reflected in the crystallization of humanitarianism in the cult of "social science." The formation of the American Social Science Association in 1868 gave institutional expression to the twin emphases which were to characterize American sociological thinking into the twentieth century: on the one hand was expressed the desire to accumulate social data in a purely scientific spirit; and on the other, the frank assertion that social science should not only study society, but should also improve it.[7] Many members of the Free Religious Association were to be found upon the rolls of the new organization, and Frank B. Sanborn, the editor of its Journal, addressed the Free Religious Association in 1868 on "The Relation of Religion to Philanthropy and Social Science." An important group among the free religionists, including Lucy Stone, the abolitionist and women's rights leader, and Horace Seaver, Kneeland's successor on the *Investigator*, would completely identify religion with humanitarianism;[8] while all agreed that the two were closely related. The theists generally concurred in Abbot's conviction that the motivating force of both free religion and reform was faith in man as a progressive being, thus establishing an organic as well as an accidental relationship between the two.[9] The infinite perfectibility of man, assured by scientific

5. *Freedom and Fellowship in Religion*, pp. 338–342.
6. Frothingham, *Recollections*, p. 74.
7. *Journal of Social Science: Containing the Transactions of the American Association*, no. 1 (June, 1869), p. 2.
8. F. R. A., *Proceedings, 1869*, pp. 99–111.
9. *The Index*, I (Jan. 15, 1870), 2.

social research, was still the ideal of free religionists and humanitarians.[10] A distinctive element in this later nineteenth-century perfectionism was its reliance upon the scientific method. In approaching social problems D. A. Wasson believed that religion was dealing with phenomena subject to the laws of outward things, for which it had no criteria enabling it to pass judgment. High principles of rectitude, honor, charity, and endeavor were in themselves no key to the solution of complex economic and social problems. To fulfill its humanitarian function religion must form intelligent opinions based upon the best systematic knowledge of social conditions.[11] Mrs. Anna Garlin Spencer would have turned the Free Religious Association into a laboratory in which to discover the laws of social progress and make practical efforts to alleviate the lot of the unfortunate.[12] The New York Sociologic Society, also dominated by active members of the Free Religious Association, adopted the imposing pseudo-scientific philosophy of Herbert Spencer in its statement of the principles governing social organization. It pronounced society to be an organism, developing by a process of differentiation and variation towards a stable social equilibrium. At the moment, the social organism was experiencing the difficult transition to a more complicated industrial system. The Sociologic Society believed that this transition could safely be made only through "a knowledge of the law of correlated interests as a *religious and economic* principle governing human development." Expressed in more familiar terms the law of correlated interests was found to be the ancient maxim: "Thou shalt make thy neighbor's welfare identical with thine own." [13]

In insisting upon the clarification and precise definition of necessary human relationships as its contribution to humanitarian reform the new social science was admitting that social problems were fundamentally moral in nature. The relevance of religion for reform immediately became clear to those who, like William J. Potter, were convinced that the Christian churches had perverted Christ's teaching of healing and redemption from the actual miseries of this life into mystical dogma and empty cere-

---

10. F. R. A., *Proceedings, 1870,* pp. 37–38.
11. D. A. Wasson, "The Relation of Social Science to Religion," F. R. A., *Proceedings, 1869,* pp. 79–92. *Freedom and Fellowship in Religion,* pp. 409–411.
12. *The Index,* n.s., II (April 13, 1882), 487–489.
13. *The Index,* n.s., IV (May 1, 8, 1884), 520, 536.

mony. All great religions, he held, had assigned a vital rôle to morality, although at the maturity of each religious system there was always a tendency towards practical separation, leading many to assume erroneously that the religious sentiment was worthless, while the moral sentiment was all-sufficient. Free religion insisted that religion furnished the base as well as the dynamic force for morality.[14] Later, in the 'nineties, many orthodox Christians were to come to the same conclusion, and in the Christian socialist movement they were to awaken the churches to a sense of their social obligations.

Finally, to become an acceptable pattern in American thinking, humanitarianism had to be more carefully defined and integrated with the dominant tradition of individualism. Here also free religion aided in developing useful formulas. Darwinian evolution, with its principle of the survival of the fittest, provided ammunition of inestimable value to "rugged individualists," or social Darwinists.[15] But these men, the great economic over-lords of the Carnegie type, and their tough-minded intellectual compatriots, like William Graham Sumner, who were prepared to accept the doctrine of the struggle for existence in the most literal sense, had no monopoly on the fair name of individualist. Another tradition, which has borne fruit of at least equal value to American culture, may be called "humanitarian individualism."

The humanitarian individualists were distinguished primarily by the conviction that the individual was the seat of spiritual values worthy of preservation and cultivation at all costs. Emerson was one of the great spokesmen of this tradition, and the free religionists carried it on into the post-Appomattox period. After Darwin had formulated his evolutionary hypothesis the two schools of individualism became more clearly distinguished, and in the latter part of the century frequently clashed. Several illuminating encounters took place within the pages of *The Index* between social Darwinists and humanitarian individualists. Both groups accepted evolution in the world of nature, while social Darwinists insisted that the principle of the "survival of the fittest" applied equally to human relations. William Graham Sumner, their chief spokesman, maintained that there could be no alternative to the survival of the fittest but the "survival of the

14. *The Index*, III (June 29, 1872), 205–206; n.s., IV (April 24, 1884), 506.
15. See Richard Hofstadter, *Social Darwinism in American Thought, 1860–1915* (Philadelphia, 1944).

unfittest." If James the Fit, through a sentimental humanitarianism, were to assist William the Unfit he would at once dissipate
the fruits of his fitness and assure the survival of the unfit, thus
effectively checking the harsh but necessary process by which
nature fashions the progress of the race. William J. Potter, on the
other hand, defined the position of humanitarian individualism
when he replied that the survival of the fittest, in the sense in
which the term applied to phenomena in the brute world, did
not pertain to problems in social ethics. The ambiguity in the
term "fitness" must first be clarified. In the brute world the term
was a purely descriptive designation of those species and individuals which had in fact survived. Where man was concerned, however, fitness immediately became invested with moral qualities.
The noblest and best *should* survive. In the rational world the
fitter could and must transform the unfit into fitness. This was
the theme of all moral teaching. Potter asserted that the principle
of evolution itself had changed as society had evolved. It was now
apparent that the problems of society ultimately resolved themselves into moral issues. The fittest for civilized existence were
the noblest and best. Natural selection had yielded a place for
sympathy and the moral sense. "The vast world process of evolution is, indeed, ennobled, when the selfish struggle for existence
is thus transformed into that power of moral personality which
is able purposely to shape results for the general benefit." He
did not mean to imply that the evolutionary principle was no
longer applicable to human life in any sense. It was still true
that hardship and suffering were nature's penalty for violating
the laws of life. Misery still inhered in vice and crime. Nor should
charity interfere with this just law of retribution. But philanthropy should turn to prevention and attack the causes of human
failure. In other words, the appearance of man in the evolutionary
process brought a new factor into play. While nature worked
blindly, man saw right and wrong. He employed foresight, with
rational and moral selection. His aim was to preserve the best, not
the strongest or the most cunning. The weak and vicious should
be transformed, and not destroyed.[16]

Professor Sumner tartly replied that there was indeed a fallacy
in applying the doctrine of the survival of the fittest to men if
the term was to be invested with moral qualities, for then the
definition was changed. Sumner evidently saw no reason why man

16. *The Index*, n.s., IV (May 22, 1884), 554.

should interpose his moral whims upon the inexorable laws of nature. Potter's alternative was but a restatement of the survival of
the unfittest. Nor was his implication that the good life assured
survival well founded, if the faculties for survival thus won were
dissipated in redeeming the unfit.[17] It was obvious by this time
that the two men no longer had a common basis for discussion.
When Potter denied that the good man imperiled his chances for
survival by aiding the bad man he was thinking in terms of moral
qualities which were incomprehensible to the thorough-going
Darwinian.[18]

The discussion was continued by other social Darwinists who
were courageous enough to deduce certain logical social consequences of the doctrine explicitly repudiating the principles of
humanitarian reform. Henry W. Holland observed that the
selection of the fittest in the struggle for life and the transmission
by inheritance of superior qualities to descendants left little room
for the progressive influence of education. Close ties of family and
race would permit at best a "modified altruism" within these
blood groups as they carried on their ceaseless competition without. The successful competitors must maintain social conditions
that assured the success and fertility of the better part of the
community, or in other words, themselves, without allowing the
process to be stultified by irenic counsels of universal brotherhood
and equality. The obvious implications of social Darwinism were
competition, war, immigration restriction, severe repression of
criminals and paupers, the fostering of agricultural rather than
of industrial classes, and above all, measures to assure the early
marriage and generous propagation of the best and dominant
classes.[19]

In contrast to this simple projection of natural selection from
biological to social evolution the humanitarian individualists insisted upon making a fundamental distinction between the two
processes. Due to man's moral and rational nature the struggle
for existence had become much milder in civilized society, becoming at best competition in the useful arts. The vast structure
of political and social institutions, essentially coöperative in nature, assists in adjusting men to the environment, and in relaxing
the severity of operation of the Malthusian formula. B. F. Under-

17. *The Index,* n.s., IV (May 29, 1884), 567.
18. *The Index,* n.s., IV (June 5, 19, 1884), 578, 603–604.
19. *The Index,* n.s., IV (January 10, 1884), 331–332.

wood drew upon Lewes and Büchner, the contemporary English and German philosophers, in searching for a naturalistic basis of morality, which he found in the sympathetic appreciation of the common weaknesses of the race. Wherever moral principles replaced to any appreciable degree the brutal struggle for life and men coöperated to mutual advantage there the influence of natural selection diminished in proportion. To nineteenth-century urban Americans it seemed reasonable to assume that as peaceful competition replaced the warlike struggle of nations, an intermingling of peoples, such as was occurring in America, with consequent uniformity of culture would spread across the globe and oppose the separation of new species. Future advance would not favor certain races at the expense of others, but would develop the species as a whole. The humanitarians believed that the social Darwinists ascribed far too strong an influence to heredity. Within obvious limits, man was much less susceptible to hereditary than to moral and environmental influences. Nor could a dispassionate view of history confirm the superiority of blood or race groups. Progress appeared rather to depend upon such equalization of the means by which the struggle for existence was carried on as would permit the full development of the talents and opportunities of all.[20]

The width of the intellectual canyon separating these traditions of individualism gave some indication of how incompatible might be the social ideas each would contribute to American culture. Rugged individualism bequeathed the dominant laissez-faire, minimum-state philosophy codified in many a speech and decision in the later nineteenth century. Humanitarian individualism, starting with the principle that the welfare of each was the concern of all, was to advocate the use of the state to preserve a healthy economic environment for the individual, as in the philosophy of Progressivism; it would appear in the panacea of Henry George to check monopoly control of land by means of the single tax; and it would be the basic presupposition underlying the theory of the general-welfare state. Free religion did much to foster humanitarian individualism by indicating its basis in an ethic of service.

The free religious philosophy of reform had to be formulated in accordance with these characteristics of American humanitar-

20. *The Index,* n.s., IV (January 10, 1884), 327–329.

ianism. The most comprehensive statement came from the pen of
Francis Abbot. It approached the subject from a rationalistic
and specifically anti-Christian point of view. It insisted that reform must preserve and guarantee a staunch individualism based
upon absolute moral values. Finally, it was sustained by the
conviction that the evolutionary process was itself moving towards
the realization of man's noblest ideals.

Although the nineteenth century was, in Abbot's opinion,
preëminently the age of humanitarian reform, the absence of a
coherent program and method indicated the need of an underlying
philosophy of reform. Certain reforms contradicted each other
flatly. Prohibition killed temperance; socialist reformers were at
the throats of trade unionists who sought to enhance the property
rights of labor; free traders rightly regarded the advocates of
coöperatives as monopolists. Each reformer claimed for his particular panacea a universal efficacy that would cure the world's
ills. The churches with their principle of spiritual subservience
and their promise of salvation in the hereafter naturally contributed nothing to worldly reform. These equally earnest but
discordant notes indicated the need of a basic principle of reform
capable of application in all directions. Free religion, with its
faith in natural evolution, proposed to formulate this principle
as "the intelligent direction of individual and social energies to
the development of a higher civilization, stimulated by undoubt-
ing confidence in the capacity of mankind to improve their own
condition indefinitely through a more complete obedience to the
laws of nature." It was not expected that the application of this
general theory of reform would immediately usher in the Golden
Age. Free religionists were not utopians. They believed that reforms were permanently achieved only as mankind came to conceive of nature as a self-evolving whole, of which man as a progressive being was a part.

Four postulates might be deduced from the conception of the
universe as a process of moral evolution. The first was the principle of individual freedom under natural law. Here free religion
announced its adherence to the dominant American creed of individualism. No reform was worthy of the name that did not rest
upon the conviction that as a rational and moral being man real-
izes his destiny only through self-mastership and obedience to
duty. But this ethical approach introduced a fundamental distinction between the free religious attitude and the implicit as-

sumptions of American practice. Reformers generally accepted
the theory that out of a conflict of interests in society an equable
adjustment amounting to a closer approximation to the general
welfare would emerge, let the ethical chips fall where they might.
The forces of propaganda and ballots were fully justified provided that the end was worthy. The nineteenth century witnessed
the gradual perfection of technique employed by what might be
called the legislative theory of reform. Free religion, on the other
hand, insisted that no reform was worthy of the name that did not
reform individuals through a process of conviction and voluntary
assent. Francis Abbot predicted the fiasco of prohibition, for
instance, sixty years before the Twenty-First Amendment. However, a reform program that could be realized only through the
transformation of individuals would hardly appeal to impatient
humanitarians whose burning sense of social injustices might
prompt them to sweep aside the barriers of privilege and greed
that barred their way.

Consistent with ethical individualism was the second principle:
"Social coöperation and universal fellowship under natural law."
United in opposition to tyranny and dedicated to self-govern-
ment under republican institutions men would be free to devote
themselves to the general good in amity and mutual helpfulness.
The principle of the moral solidarity of mankind followed
directly. Society and the individual should be mutually dedicated
to one another. By implication racial and national distinctions
must eventually be merged in a common humanity. Finally, the
criterion of reform was to be the harmonious adjustment of individual and social relations according to the laws of the universe.
Abbot held these laws to be inherent in man's nature, emerging to
consciousness as the moral and intellectual capacities developed.
Since a healthy existence could be achieved only in conformity
with natural law, reform was identical with the science of society.
Virtue and knowledge must go hand in hand. Once these principles were generally recognized and acted upon all desirable reform would be realized, for they alone approached the fundamentals of all evil, ignorance and selfishness.[21]

True reform was to be achieved only through a closer approximation to the social principles and organization required by the
laws of nature at the particular moment in the evolutionary

21. *The Index,* III (November 2, 9, 16, 23, 30, 1872), 352–353, 360–361, 368–369,
376, 384–385.

process. The free religious conception of social evolution was derived largely from Herbert Spencer. The theory would seem to have demanded for its application a meticulous science of history in order to set forth the precise requirements of a just social order in the nineteenth century. Yet Spencer's righteous strictures upon the iniquities of the age were based upon voluminous studies dealing with almost everything else but social history, while his American disciples were content with vague references to social law and especially moral values. John Fiske alone of the evolutionary-naturalist group undertook extensive historical studies. His lectures on *American Political Ideas Viewed from the Standpoint of Universal History*[22] traced the successful efforts of northwestern Europeans and Americans to achieve an equilibrium between freedom and authority. Free religionists were generally in agreement with this approach to historical problems, although they gradually discovered that they differed widely among themselves in their conceptions of the institutional and economic bases of freedom.

Reforms enabling the individual and society to conform more closely to the laws of nature and the evolutionary process could be achieved only through universal education. The free religious emphasis upon education was consistent with the innate conservatism of the group. Education meant nothing less than the full development of rational and spiritual powers. Abbot was realistic enough to recognize the inadequacy of formal schooling, no matter how highly developed. The home must remain a far more important educational institution than the school. Life itself must be understood as an educational experience, to which political, industrial, scientific, artistic, and even recreational institutions must all contribute. The spirit of reform, once firmly rooted, could be expected to provide a certain impetus of its own, and Abbot quoted with approval the pungent comment of Col. Higginson: "Seeing the educational value to this generation of the reforms for which it has contended, and especially of the anti-slavery enterprise, one must feel an impulse of pity for our successors, who seem likely to have no convictions for which they can honestly be mobbed." That Abbot was conscious of the paradox of placing Higginson's reference to the educational value of abolition on the same page with his own reasons for distrusting

22. Fiske, *American Political Ideas* (New York and London, 1899), lectures originally delivered at the Royal Institution of Great Britain in May, 1880.

reforms secured by means of ballots is unlikely, since he was convinced that transformation of the hearts and minds of men must precede the altering of institutions.[23]

The principles of social reform as stated by Abbot were largely acceptable in free religious circles, but differences of emphasis and application that developed as many members turned their attention during the late 'seventies and 'eighties to social problems made it clear that there could be no common free religious program of reform. Conservative as the practical implications of Abbot's emphasis upon education as the means of reform were, they scarcely compared with D. A. Wasson's yearning for a return of the old Federalist days. Wasson criticized the doctrine of inalienable rights as used to justify unrestrained individualism. He agreed with the socialists that the individual's rights and obligations stem from the social nexus, and are not anterior to it. But this repudiation of natural rights smacked more of William Graham Sumner than of socialism. Assuming that it was the function of a civilized society to perfect standards of justice the question remained as to the method of achieving these goals. Wasson believed that representative government based upon the suffrage of wise and foolish alike concentrated altogether too much power in the civil state. The new ideal of equality, "long since become spurious by excess," if fully realized in the form of socialism would bring with it "poverty, servitude, and barbarism." Certain equality of rights, such as protection of property and person, access to the courts, and education, must be maintained. But there could be no equal right of function irrespective of capacity and fitness to make the function serviceable. Wasson's social thinking, typical of the transcendentalist wing of free religion, had little in common with the prevailing non-qualitative thought of the Gilded Age. His practical conclusions were consistent with the reigning individualism, although his sense of social values revealed his understanding of the hollowness of its pretensions. But his fear of mediocrity largely stalemated the reformism implicit in his individualist values.[24]

In the 'eighties, however, the need for practical reform that had always been advocated by certain younger members of the Association received added impetus from new members who demanded that social questions receive greater consideration in their

23. *The Index*, III (December 7, 14, 1872), 392, 400–401.
24. *The Index*, III (February 10, 1872), 41–44.

discussions and activities. R. Heber Newton, the prominent Episcopalian clergyman, helped to launch the Christian socialist movement in America when he addressed the Association in 1885 on the religious aspect of socialism. Reformers who sensed the similarities between socialist enthusiasm and the religious spirit were obliged to explain the paradox of the practically universal identification of socialism with religious unbelief. These reformers were the first among the Protestants to measure the signficance of the defection from the churches of large sections of the working class.[25] Newton attributed to the miseries of the existing order the prevalent disbelief in a beneficent providence. He discovered from history, however, that periods of great religious vitality were always accompanied by movements for social reorganization. Similarly, he noted a historic tendency for social aspiration to kindle into religion. These associations could be explained only on the assumption that the Kingdom of God was not an illusion, "but the Divine Order slowly coming forth upon our human society." Newton here touched the cardinal theological doctrinc of thc Social Gospel movement.

The establishment of the Kingdom upon earth was not to be consummated in any catastrophic day of judgment, as more naive Christians had once expected, nor through violent revolution, as many socialist reformers predicted. Our understanding of the historical and social process had taught us to appreciate the desirability of gradual evolutionary change. "Sane" socialists, according to Newton, preferred an orderly transition to a socialized society. This reliance upon a "uniformitarian" conception of social evolution was to become a characteristic feature of American liberal thought. Thus Newton warned those whose religious sense naturally aroused sympathy for socialism not to plunge ahead blindly. Too rapid progress even on the right road spelled disaster. Nature after all moved slowly. While he would not argue that the French revolution had been a catastrophe without redeeming features it was at least the regrettable result of a previous enforced stoppage of progress. In religious terms, the millennium remained an ultimate hope rather than an immediate possibility.[26]

While the humanitarian faith found its place within these

25. See James Dombrowski, *The Early Days of Christian Socialism in America* (New York, 1936).
26. *The Index,* n.s., V (June 25, 1885), 617–622.

limits it gradually became more conscious of evils which could hardly be solved in terms of individual morality. By 1885, Potter, the last of the founders to remain active in the Association, was prepared to question the defensibility of a society that permitted the amount of poverty so painfully evident in industrial America. Men could scarcely be bound by moral obligations if the structure of their society were such that many of them had no alternatives but beggary and crime on the one hand and starvation on the other. "That there is danger here which stares the proud and complacent nineteenth century in the face, it were folly to be so optimistic as to refuse to see." Unless opportunities for happiness and advancement were open to all, modern civilization was doomed to perish. Nevertheless, two principles must underlie any plan of social reorganization. Competition, insofar as it made for self-reliance, must have a place in any practicable theory of socialism. The family, in the second place, must be preserved as the best means of securing the affectional and moral interests of mankind. Potter anticipated that no very revolutionary changes could occur without affecting these institutions; but, after all, was not the greatest need "a new baptism of human society into the spirit of the old commandment, 'Love thy neighbor as thyself,' or a revival in the human heart of the ancient and well-nigh universal sentiment of the Golden Rule?" [27] In 1879, Frothingham, Adler, and Heber Newton had joined Frederick Law Olmsted and E. L. Godkin in creating the Coöperative Colony Aid Association of New York, the purpose of which was to assist agricultural groups, especially immigrants, in establishing coöperative communities in the West. At least one colony was planted in Salina County, Kansas. In its aims and methods, however, the project harked back to the abortive community movement of pre-Civil War days, rather than forward to the coöperatives of the twentieth century.[28] This was the limit of free religious reform in the area of economic institutions.

The interpretation of the important events of the Gilded Age provided a handy index to the gradual crystallization of a characteristic social attitude in free religion. Preoccupied at first with its program of religious reform the great strikes of 1877 rudely awakened free religion, and at the same time revealed the social

27. *The Index*, n.s., VI (August 6, 1885), 62.
28. *The Index*, n.s., I (July 22, 1880), 43–44.

conservatism of its adherents. Francis Abbot condemned the railroad strikes as riot, an inexcusable destruction of the moral order. His strictures revealed a certain uneasiness, however, in the obligation which he felt to explain the distinction between such riots and incidents like the Boston Tea Party, which, as part of a larger revolutionary movement aimed to establish morality on a firmer foundation, were entirely justifiable. The essence of modern civilization lay in freedom of contract, and to supersede its operation by violent means was nothing less than anarchy. He was prepared to admit the prevailing selfish lust for profits, the inequable and unjust distribution of wealth, and the legitimate grievances of labor. But the remedy of these defects for which all sane people prayed could not avert the over-production and consequent fall of wages that was inherent in the existing state of industrial technology. There could certainly be no solution of the industrial problem that disregarded equal rights.[29] The reactions of other members of the Association ranged from red-baiting conservatism to socialism and philosophical anarchism of the Josiah Warren stamp.[30]

In the following decade conservative free religion gradually reconciled itself to the téchniques of organized labor, although it had difficulty in accepting such features as the boycott, closed shop, and sympathetic strike.[31] In branding these practices as tyranny free religion showed its reluctance to abandon the old individualistic morality for the new corporate conception of rights.

The political attitudes of the free religious leaders suffered similar dislocations in the rapid changes after the Civil War. Nearly all of the founders of the Association had been radical Republicans, closely allied with abolitionist reformers. The Association itself had been formed during the great wave of humanitarian enthusiasm that followed the freeing of the slaves. Ten years later, however, there was much to challenge the complacence of Republican reformers. The more thoughtful among them realized that the great wave of zeal with which the victorious North had undertaken to reform Southern life and institutions in order to establish equal rights for white and black men according to

29. *The Index,* VIII (August 2, 1877), 366–367.
30. *The Index,* VIII (August 9, 16, 30, October 11, December 6, 1877), 379–380, 392–393, 416, 488–489, 583; IX (January 10, February 14, 1878), 17, 80–81.
31. *The Index,* n.s., VI (April 22, May 13, 1886), 506–507, 542–543.

ideal democratic principles had failed.[32] They listened with approval when an intelligent Negro, Archibald H. Grimké, told
them that their reconstruction program had failed in spite of its
high principles because their party had thought only in terms of
political rights, and because it had been hasty, vindictive, and unscientific. Nothing short of complete reëducation, to use a modern
term, could have brought the radical ideal to fruition.[33] It was
a similar analysis to that which had suggested to Abbot the importance of education as the basis of reform, and that prompted
him to launch the abortive Conscience party.

The corrupt politics of the Gilded Age was naturally revolting
to liberals who insisted that a healthy social life must be rooted
in sound morality. The strain of pessimism running through the
era was reflected in an occasional address or in the motives that
must have prompted Abbot to reprint in *The Index* an article by
Francis Parkman on "The Failure of Universal Suffrage." [34]
The historian attributed the uneasiness of the age to a growing
realization that the great panacea of universal suffrage, far from
improving the tone of public life, was actually debasing it by
assuring the rule of mediocrity. But when President Grant suggested that suffrage be restricted by constitutional amendment
to those who could read and write Abbot protested that it was
the genius of true republicanism to give the best possible education to all and to exclude no class from the suffrage. Similarly,
the men of the Association usually gave loyal support to their
prominent female colleagues in the perennial campaign to secure
women's suffrage.[35]

With an immediate concern for social reform asserted to be a
prime object of free religion it was inevitable that the official
policy of the Association on the matter should be a live issue. We
have said enough about the attitudes of its leaders, however, to
indicate the difficulties to be overcome if an active political and
economic reform program were to be undertaken. While the Executive Committee debated the specific religious activities which
the Association should undertake, a demand from the more radical
wing for positive social action was heard. Julia Ward Howe led

32. *The Index,* IX (February 21, 1878), 86–89.
33. *The Index,* n.s., VII (July 1, 1886), 5.
34. *The Index,* IX (August 15, 1878), 386–388, 391–392. *The North American
Review,* CCLXIII (July–August, 1878), 1–20.
35. *The Index,* n.s., I (September 2, 1880), 115; n.s., IV (April 17, 1884), 499–
500.

the attack at the Annual Meeting in 1869, charging the Association with being a featureless abstraction, a belief without a church, because it was devoting its energies to speculation and avoiding positive religious action. Aaron M. Powell, a prominent peace advocate, took Mrs. Howe's cue, suggesting that an organization uniting differing faiths should find its natural outlet in humanitarian activity. What, for instance, did the Association propose to do about the Negro problem? Lucy Stone and Horace Seaver echoed the same note.[36]

The drive of the activists resulted in a crystallization of opinion in the Executive Committee, with the first announcement of a general policy at the meeting in 1870. On the religious side the committee felt that the character of free religion as the common basis of all special faiths had been sufficiently emphasized, even to the extent of creating the impression that the Association had no aim of its own aside from providing a platform for warring sects. In the future the positive aspects of free religion should be stressed. In the social field the committee recognized consideration of pressing political and economic problems of American life as within the purview of the Association. The relation of religion to the political state and to the public schools needed more careful definition and regulation. Legally established Christianity, in the form of Sunday laws, legal oaths, and the qualifications of jurors and witnesses, must be abolished. The practical implications of the latest findings in science and philosophical speculation must be demonstrated. Certain social evils, such as the inequitable adjustment obtaining between capital and labor, women's rights, pauperism, crime, intemperance, and racial problems, must be attacked. Here was a plan for action ambitious enough to satisfy the most ardent reformer.[37]

With the decision taken in 1873, however, that the work of the Association should be confined to that of a general agitation society, the possibility of a program of active social work vanished. Those who remained loyal to the Association were devoted to its religious ideals, while the active humanitarians tended to lose interest. William Lloyd Garrison criticized the Association because it was not zealous enough.[38] The Reverend J. M. L. Babcock, editor of *The New Age*, announced in 1876 that he was be-

36. F. R. A., *Proceedings, 1869*, pp. 48–50, 60, 69, 100, 110.
37. F. R. A., *Proceedings, 1870*, pp. 10–12.
38. F. R. A., *Proceedings, 1879*, p. 12.

coming bored with free religious piety. The centennial year saw
rampant political corruption and industrial depression. Yet the
Free Religious Association must discuss abstractions in scholarly
style while a million men tramped the highways unemployed.
Babcock demanded practical attention to social and political
regeneration.[39] Finally, with the resignation of Felix Adler in
1882 the last effort to commit the Association to social-welfare
work failed.

The refusal to commit organized free religion to an active
program of reform did not mean, however, that radicalism was
repudiating its pledge to better the lot of man. The decision of
the Association not to participate in active work was considered
to be merely a matter of the most advisable division of labor.
Potter indicated the difficulty which prevented the Association
from coöperating in active work. The central idea of the Association was the application of free thought to religious problems,
with the consequent emancipation of religious belief and life from
allegiance to all authority save that of truth as determined by
rational human intelligence. The application of such a fundamental principle would necessarily eventuate in various types of
practical activity: some would wage war on sect and irrational
dogma; others would live practical lives governed by spiritual
freedom; some would proclaim the sympathy of religions and
declare the common postulates underlying special faiths to be a
universal religion; others would work for the complete separation
of church and state, and for the secular character of the Constitution; and still others would ignore church and theology and devote themselves to free spiritual and moral education. With such
a diversity of interest arising out of the free religious ideal, agreement upon a program of activity would naturally be difficult.[40]
Nevertheless, in addition to the recognition of its social obligations, free religion did actively promote a few minor reforms in
matters which had an immediate connection with the liberation of
religious life.

The mid-nineteenth century Sabbath, sanctified by all the stern
traditions of American Protestantism, was a formidable weekly
interlude when, as Emerson's Aunt Mary said, even nature looked
like a pulpit.[41] The free religionists proposed to humanize the

39. F. R. A., *Proceedings, 1876*, p. 18.
40. F. R. A., *Proceedings, 1876*, pp. 14–15.
41. Emerson, *Journals*, IX, p. 312.

Sabbath by making it a holiday for rest, recreation, and spiritual cultivation. Every day should be kept holy; and to reverence Sunday above Tuesday or Friday was, according to Abbot, pure superstition.[42] In 1869, the Association published an appeal in the newspapers for funds to maintain a reading room in Boston which would remain open on Sundays. All public libraries at that time were closed on the Sabbath. Presumably influential persons feared the effects of a free religious reading room, for immediately the Boston Y.M.C.A. and the Public Library announced that they would remain open throughout the week. The appeal for funds met with such poor response that the project was dropped, but the Association felt that it had won the substance of victory.[43]

The power behind the old Sabbath was the church, and free religion attacked the church at the point which assured its survival as a vested institution, namely, its right to hold property free of taxes. The first tract published by the Association was written by James Parton, the biographer, on *The Taxation of Church Property*. Parton attacked exemption on the ground that it could not be reconciled with the one intelligent principle of exemptions, namely, that whatever property the state favored with tax exemption ought to support the state. Taxation, he jested, would kill off many churches lacking the strength to die a natural death. Parton's chief purpose, however, was to point to the danger of the rapidly growing Catholic Church, constantly absorbing more property, and strengthening itself for the day when it could seriously challenge the ideal of freedom. Ecclesiastical tax exemption fostered such dangerous developments, and denied the free principle that "every tub should stand on its own bottom." [44]

The Association returned to these ecclesiastical reforms in the 'eighties, when it discovered a technique which gave free religion at least some brief publicity. The Executive Committee had been instructed by the Association in 1884 to agitate for the protection of witnesses in court from disqualification because of religious disbelief. Two petitions were presented to the Massachusetts legislature, one demanding the repeal of these disabilities, and the

42. Abbot, *The Sunday Question* . . . (Toledo, Ohio, 1869), pp. 13–16.

43. F. R. A., *Proceedings, 1869,* pp. 13–14. Potter, *The Free Religious Association,* pp. 19–20.

44. James Parton, *The Taxation of Church Property.* (Free Religious Tracts, no. 1. Boston, 1873).

other requesting the taxation of church property. Both petitions were rejected, but the preliminary hearings received considerable attention in the papers, and the Association realized that here was a useful method of spreading its ideas. A lawyer employed by the Association discovered that a court decision preventing the collection of damages from fraud arising out of transactions made on Sunday was still in force. The precedent was found, appropriately enough, in a case involving a horse trade. The lawyer also discovered that anyone purchasing property on Sunday might keep it without payment.[45] A further petition pointing to these anomalies was presented to the legislature, and was rejected by it in 1886.[46] The attack upon these vestiges of older days did not, however, restore the waning vitality of the Association.

The insistence of free religion that philanthropy and social reform were an integral part of religious faith, although not realized in practice by the Free Religious Association as an organization, was at least the first consistent assertion that spiritual needs and social opportunities are inseparably united. It was an expression of the activist and reformist spirit of nineteenth-century American social democracy. It also inaugurated the period of organized religious philanthropy and reform. The educational ideas of free religion were incorporated in the Ethical Culture schools of Felix Adler, while its reform program was taken up by the Social Gospel, Christian Socialist, and church-settlement movements.

45. F. R. A., Proceedings, 1885, *The Index,* n.s., V (June 4, 1885), 583–585.
46. F. R. A., Proceedings, 1886, *The Index,* n.s., VI (June 3, 1886), 583–584.

# VIII

## THE SIGNIFICANCE OF FREE RELIGION

LINDSAY SWIFT'S comment on Brook Farm, that "there was a distinct beginning, a fairly coherent progress, but a vague termination," applies equally to the free religious movement. The history of the Free Religious Association has not been completed within the limits of this study, for the Association lived on into the twentieth century, far beyond the days of its importance or usefulness. The concern of free religion with social problems, tentatively asserted in the nineteenth century, became the dominant note in more recent times, when the Association was no longer in the van of religious thought, in this or in other respects. Its contributions were made in the third and fourth quarters of the last century, and with the World Parliament of Religions, symbolizing both its success and its failure, the useful period of the Association's life came to a close.

After some twenty years of effort to weld religious liberalism into an organized or at least consciously coherent movement, W. J. Potter summarized the factors which had in a great measure combined to nullify his labors.[1] First and most important was the spirit of individualism, a tendency characteristic of religious radicalism since the Reformation, springing from insistence upon the right of individual inquiry and judgment. In America the tradition of religious freedom served to remove apprehension of ecclesiastical dominance, thus making liberal organization for purely defensive reasons apparently unnecessary. Certain characteristics of liberalism as an attitude of mind also rendered it singularly unsuited to organized activity. As a philosophy of spiritual individualism its common affirmations had of necessity to partake of a critical rather than a constructive nature. Liberal action was further impeded by the widespread conviction that sound progress came about inevitably through general enlightenment rather than by requiring any means of special organization. Liberalism felt itself poised on the crest of the wave, surging on to new shores with the inexorable drift of things. Potter insisted that while liberal

1. *The Index*, n.s., IV (Feb. 7, 1884), 374.

religion could not have a common creed it should have a common philosophy, forgetting that the common philosophy was buried in the unspoken assumptions of the time. Beyond these inherent defects of liberalism certain unfortunate circumstances conspired to discredit it. The anti-Christian cult of the mid-nineteenth century, because its reaction from the dogmatic creedalism of the churches paralleled that of free religion, was frequently confused with it. This similarity hurt the agnostic more than the theistic wing of the free religious group. More annoying was the ease with which liberalism was used as a mask to shield licentiousness. The undermining of Abbot's Liberal League by the distributors of pornography who wished to use the League for the repeal of the Comstock laws was a harsh experience for the radicals. They had already been accused of promoting infidelity and free love, and the fate of the Liberal Leagues was all the confirmation needed for hostile eyes.

Despite these factors, which, for all practical purposes, nullified efforts to organize free religion, the ideas of the group contributed to break down the narrow ecclesiastical authoritarianism which characterized mid-nineteenth-century Protestantism. Because the churches had refused to compromise their literally interpreted creeds by conceding the truth of the rationalist cosmology, the radicals were able to put the issue in the light of a conflict between freedom and authority. On such terms the results were inevitable. T. DeWitt Talmadge, one of the most popular evangelicals of the day, who specialized in ridiculing his opponents, was himself made ridiculous by Minot Savage when he attempted to laugh the evolutionists off the American scene.[2] Savage insisted that the scientist was the truly religious man, and that the priest was the infidel when he resisted the indisputable findings of science. The American clergy were so far convinced of the practical wisdom of Savage's opinion that the Belgian theologian, Count Goblet d'Alviella, who studied religious conditions in America in the decade of the 1880's, discovered that sermons were placing far more emphasis on morals than on theology.[3] The rise of the humanitarian preacher of the Beecher type, which was by no means the product of free religion alone, marked the disintegration of the dominant evangelical Protestantism in the large cities.

2. M. J. Savage, *Evolution and Religion from the Standpoint of One who Believes in Both* (Philadelphia, 1886), p. 19 and passim.
3. Goblet d'Alviella, *The Contemporary Evolution of Religious Thought*, p. 203.

The radicals made one contribution to American religious thought, however, which became most useful to liberal Protestantism at the end of the century. The free religious movement has been discussed in these pages primarily as an attempt to save religion from an outmoded dogmatism. Most of the energies of its adherents were devoted to that end. Yet it was also a counterattack upon scepticism on behalf of the religious values which the Christian churches appeared to be in no condition to defend. The great group of the unchurched was growing rapidly throughout the nineteenth century, and it was to this group that free religion made its first appeal. From this point of view it is not surprising that the Free Religious Association made no effort to enlist the powerful support of Colonel Bob Ingersoll, America's arch infidel. Ingersoll's services in popularizing the implications of scientific thought for orthodox theology were admittedly great, but his criticism was destructive, and he could offer his followers nothing but a vague, unoriented humanism. Even B. F. Underwood, one of the leading non-theists of the free religious group, admitted that Ingersoll knew nothing of scientific or philosophical matters, and that his criticisms of the Christian cosmology were based upon Voltaire and Paine, rather than upon Darwin and Spencer.[4] All free religionists, whether they were agnostics or liberal Unitarians, were bent on the preservation of religious values, and their basic defense rested upon the empirical evidence furnished by the great religions. In this sense Abbot's dictum that human nature was the root of religion bore fruit in the influential religious thinking of William James at the end of the century, and became one of the bulwarks of Protestant modernism.

The general process of liberalization in the Protestant churches at the end of the century cannot be reviewed here; nor can the weight of the free religious influence in that development possibly be estimated. To one aspect of the disintegration of Protestant denominationalism, however, the Free Religious Association made an important contribution. It pioneered in attacking denominational and creedal exclusiveness through its emphasis upon the universality of the religious sentiment. The spectacle of representatives of several denominations and religions meeting upon the free religious platform in 1867 and frequently thereafter, each indicating the relation of his own faith to universal religion, was new in American religious life. The larger Protestant groups in ex-

4. *The Index,* n.s., IV (May 29, 1884), 568.

panding their religious horizons began to discover the extent of
their common traditions and values. A Conference of Christian
Churches, representing several denominations, was held at Hart-
ford in 1885, an event which scarcely could have taken place before the Civil War. Nor was the new community of spirit confined
to the Protestant Christian churches. A great interest in the
Oriental religions swept the country in the last two decades of the
century, creating a wide demand for lectures and literature on
those faiths.[5] The movement culminated in the World Parliament
of Religions, when the Indian and Chinese representatives received national attention. It was true that out of this increased
sympathy and understanding for alien religions there did not
occur a popular trend toward free religion, as the radicals had
wished, but the impact of the new tendencies upon Protestantism
were undeniable.

Free religion was most immediately influential in the transformation of Unitarianism from a Christocentric religion to a prag-
matic, humanistic theism, retaining the Christian name but
actually being Christian only in the sense of recognizing its
dependence upon the religious patterns of Western culture. The
free religious revolt in 1867 constituted a serious threat to
Unitarianism. A majority of the abler young men were openly
hostile to denominational developments, even if they did not go
with Abbot and Frothingham to the extent of abandoning the
denominational fellowship. The early meetings of the Free Religious Association easily overshadowed the activities of Unitarianism. The aggressive attack of the new organization upon the
larger problems of American religious and social life gave its
platform a national importance never attained by Unitarian
denominational activity. Edward Everett Hale, who had aided Dr.
Bellows in planning the Convention of 1865 in order to outmaneu-
ver the "Sadduceeish or sceptical brethren," [6] was sufficiently
alarmed at the defection to choke back his distaste for radicalism
and extend the hand of reconciliation in the form of a curious
amendment offered at the Unitarian National Conference in 1868:

To secure the largest unity of the spirit and the widest practical
coöperation, it is hereby understood that all the declarations of this

5. *The Index*, n.s., V (June 4, 1885), 578.
6. E. E. Hale, Jr., *The Life and Letters of Edward Everett Hale* (2 vols.,
Boston, 1917), II, 12.

Conference, including the preamble and constitution, are expressions only of its majority, and dependent wholly for their effect upon the consent they command on their own merits from the churches here represented or belonging within the circle of our fellowship.[7]

The hope that such a gesture might lure the rebels back into the denominational fold showed little understanding of the temper of radicalism. The free religionists returned to the denomination only when the old sectarianism had been destroyed. The liberalizing of the Unitarian fellowship progressed so rapidly that by 1880 Sidney Morse and E. C. Towne were convinced that Abbot's Syracuse preamble would then be acceptable to the denomination.[8] In 1882 Minot Savage offered an amendment to the constitution of the Unitarian National Conference which virtually secured freedom of thought within the denomination. The amendment stated that while the constitution embodied the views of a majority of Unitarians, it was distinctly understood that there was no authoritative test of Unitarianism, and that none would be excluded from its fellowship "who, while differing from us in belief, are in general sympathy with our purposes and practical aims." [9] In accepting the amendment Unitarians were tacitly admitting that the Lordship of Christ had become a dead letter. Abbot and Potter spurned this negative commitment, hoping for a positive pledge of allegiance to spiritual freedom, but the majority of free religionists gradually returned to the Unitarian fold.

During his declining years Octavius Frothingham took his place again in the family pew of the First Church in Boston, where as a boy he had listened to his father. The Unitarianism to which he returned in 1890 was a far different faith from that which he had deserted in 1865. It was now more rationalistic, more socially minded, and more democratic. Its Lockean and transcendental emphases had given way to historical and empirical foundations.

It ignored the bounds of Scripture and even Christianity, having become a vague form of theism, interpreting spiritual experience according to the accepted standards of scientific and philosophical thought. Its doctrine of God was now rational, scientific, human, and adapted to the needs of the highest spirituality. Its belief in immortality was held as a hope, a consola-

7. Cooke, *Unitarianism*, p. 205.
8. *Farewell Dinner to Francis Ellingwood Abbot, on Retiring from the Editorship of the "Index"* . . . (Boston, 1880), pp. 32, 37.
9. Goblet d'Alviella, *The Contemporary Evolution of Religious Thought*, p. 195.

tion, an incitement, and a reasonable inference from evolution and the spiritual nature of man. It saw the moral law inwrought in the nature of things, and attested by the highest experience of mankind.[10]

Before his death in 1879 John Weiss had seen the tendency of Unitarianism to move slowly towards liberalism. He remarked that the radicals of 1865 had been killed off in order that their doctrines might later be safely preached within the denomination. Minot Savage, who was preaching precisely those doctrines in Unitarian pulpits, conceded the truth of this observation when he traced Weiss's career in the annals of the Unitarian ministry. "The process of killing them off," he admitted, "had opened the eyes and broadened the minds of the community, and so I was enjoying a freedom which their martyrdom had purchased." [11]

10. Frothingham, *Boston Unitarianism*, pp. 259, 266.
11. M. J. Savage, in Eliot, ed., *Heralds*, III, 387–389.

# BIBLIOGRAPHICAL NOTE

## CHAPTER I

It is surprising that a denomination which for so long embraced a large portion of the intellectual aristocracy of America has not produced a denominational history worthy of the secular histories written by many of its distinguished laymen. The best general survey of Unitarianism is that by George Willis Cooke, *Unitarianism in America* (Boston, 1902), a typical denominational history, sketching the institutional and dogmatic outlines. Studies fixing the relation of Channing to the main stream of Unitarian thought, and weighing the influence of transcendentalism upon Unitarianism, have yet to appear. Special studies of Unitarian theology during the years of the transcendental and free religious revolts are Joseph H. Allen, *Our Liberal Movement in Theology* (Boston, 1882); the same author's *Sequel to "Our Liberal Movement"* (Boston, 1897); and John White Chadwick, *The Old and New Unitarian Belief* (Boston, 1894). These writers represented the new liberal Unitarianism purged by the fires of free religion, and their task was to lick old wounds. Since they emphasize denominational unity the unwary reader will never suspect the hatred and bitterness which characterized the disputed years, dogging Parker and Abbot to their graves.

In his later and more placid years O. B. Frothingham turned to Unitarian antiquities, and through the life of his father analyzed the spirit of the denomination, in *Boston Unitarianism, 1820–1850: A Study of the Life and Work of Nathaniel Langdon Frothingham* (New York and London, 1890). This is one of the most sensitive and penetrating studies in Unitarianism. The sketch which Frothingham included of the typical Unitarian layman, Peter Chardon Brooks, his maternal grandfather, deserves to become a classic, and has provided material for several recent popularizers. Frothingham was more concerned to portray a particular type of Unitarianism which he knew intimately than to analyze the main stream of Unitarian thought between Channing and Parker. To treat adequately this uncharted period of Unitarianism would require a study of the leading divines, of whom I have selected those who seemed to me to be the most characteristic. Orville Dewey's *Discourses and Reviews upon Questions in Controversial Theology and Practical Religion,* in *Works,* Vol. III (New York, 1868), typifies the evangelical Unitarianism which also produced Andrews Norton's famous *Evidences.* Because of his strategic rôle in the crystallization of Unitarian denominationalism I have used Henry W. Bellows' *Restatements of Christian Doctrine, in Twenty-five Sermons* (New York, 1860) to illustrate Unitarian orthodoxy.

The most detailed and colorful account of the Unitarian Convention of 1865 is E. C. Towne, *Unitarian Fellowship and Liberty: An Open Letter to Henry W. Bellows* (Cambridge, Mass., 1866), a biased but useful pamphlet.

Of use throughout have been the free religious and Unitarian periodicals. *The Index* was founded by Francis Abbot in 1870 and was published as a weekly at Toledo, Ohio, until 1873, when it was moved to Boston. In 1880 the Index Association presented the magazine to the Free Religious Association, which continued to publish it until 1886, when it was discontinued. The Unitarian *Christian Examiner* and *Christian Register* appeared throughout the period. The *Examiner* was a monthly review of high intellectual quality containing many articles by the radicals before the break in 1867. The *Register* was a weekly containing much incidental news of denominational life. Sidney Morse's *Radical,* published from 1865 to 1872, contains many articles by the free religionists.

## CHAPTER II

O. B. Frothingham's *Transcendentalism in New England* (New York, 1876) is still the best general history of that movement. Written during busy days at the height of the author's public career, it is an outline of what might have been a great book. Frothingham enjoyed a unique advantage as a student—he had belonged to the movement himself, eventually outgrowing rather than rejecting it. Fortunately for the present study the book is best on the religious side.

Biographical sketches of nearly all of the Unitarian and radical leaders of the period, with fairly complete bibliographies may be found in the third volume of S. A. Eliot, ed., *Heralds of a Liberal Faith* (3 vols., Boston, 1910). No extensive studies of the leaders of the free religious movement have been made. With the exception of F. E. Abbot's papers materials for such studies have probably disappeared.

Frothingham capped his voluminous literary efforts with a volume of *Recollections and Impressions* (New York, 1891). The book was written by an infirm old man. While supplying some useful factual material, it is inaccurate and appears to have been put together hastily and without the use of diaries or notes. Frothingham's intellectual migration, on the other hand, can be traced in his long list of published writings: histories, memoirs, biographies, essays, and some dozen volumes of printed sermons. Particular items used are cited in the bibliography and notes.

The extensive papers of Francis Abbot, consisting of journals, manuscript sermons, correspondence, and reprints are in the possession of his daughter, Mrs. Ralph G. Wells, of Needham, Massachusetts. Additional materials relating to *The Index* are in the hands of Abbot's son, Dr. E. Stanley Abbot, of Boston. I am indebted to Mrs. Wells and Dr. Abbot both for permission to use the papers and for much personal information. Autobiographical references are scattered through Abbot's controversial writings. *Universal Religion,* XI, no. 9 (December 1903), is a memorial number consisting of addresses in appreciation of Abbot's career.

For the life of T. W. Higginson the published materials are extensive. Mary T. Higginson, *Thomas Wentworth Higginson: the Story of his Life* (Boston, 1914); also her edition of *The Letters and Journals of Thomas Wentworth Higginson* (Boston, 1921); T. W. Higginson, *Cheerful Yesterdays* (Boston and New York, 1898); and *Part of a Man's Life* (Boston and New York, 1905). Curiously, these volumes tend to ignore Higginson's participation in the Free Religious Association, of which he was successively director, vice-president, and president (1894–1899). Materials relating to John Weiss are scanty, the best sketches being those by Frothingham in the *Unitarian Review and Religious Magazine,* XXIX (May, 1888), 417–429; and by C. A. Bartol, *Principles and Portraits* (Boston, 1880), pp. 386–412. The faithful Frothingham wrote a memoir of D. A. Wasson which, with a short autobiographical sketch, prefaces Wasson's *Essays: Religious, Social, Political* (Boston, 1889). Samuel Longfellow wrote a sympathetic memoir of Samuel Johnson to accompany the latter's *Lectures, Essays, and Sermons* (Boston, 1883).

The issues of the Syracuse Conference were debated by J. F. Clarke and F. E. Abbot, *The Battle of Syracuse: Two Essays* (Boston, 1884).

## CHAPTER III

Although the Free Religious Association is still officially in existence, it has held no meetings since 1923. The president, the Reverend George Grover Mills, describes its present condition as one of "suspended animation." During this period of somnolence the records have disappeared almost completely. Fortunately, the chief activity of the Association, its annual meetings, were reported verbatim in the *Annual Proceedings of the Free Religious Association,* which were published, together with the Annual Reports of the Executive Committee, in pamphlet form, at Boston, from 1867 to 1879. (The *First Annual Report of the Executive Committee,* Boston, 1868, was issued separately.) From 1880 to 1886, inclusive, the *Proceedings* were published serially in *The Index;* again in pamphlet form in 1887; from 1888–1892 they appeared, but not verbatim, in the *New Ideal;* again as pamphlets from 1893 to 1914, with the exception of the years 1903 to 1906, when nothing was printed. A complete file may be found in the library of the Unitarian Historical Society in Boston. The Annual Reports are valuable sources of information concerning the activities of the Association in the interim between annual meetings, and for the hopes and disappointments of its leaders. Secretary Potter, the Association's most active worker, wrote the Reports from 1868 to 1882.

Other publications of the Association included six Free Religious Tracts; a volume of essays by leading members and friends entitled *Freedom and Fellowship in Religion* (Boston, 1875); *Prophets of Liberalism* (Boston, 1900), a group of commemorative essays; and W. J. Potter's *The Free Religious Association, its Twenty-five Years and Their Meaning* (Boston, 1892), which furnishes much information on the preliminary conferences preceding the formation of the Association.

## CHAPTER IV

One reason why free religion failed to make itself clear to its contemporaries was the absence of a popular and explicit statement explaining its nature as a rationalistic and humanistic movement dedicated to the spiritual and material welfare of man, out of which the theistic or secular beliefs of its adherents might grow unimpeded.

Much labor was spent in the early years of the Association in explaining its mission, without great success. The *Annual Proceedings* of the Association for the first half dozen years contain many addresses by the officers explaining its function. (See Frothingham, in F.R.A., *Proceedings, 1868,* pp. 19–23; Potter, in F.R.A., *Proceedings, 1870,* pp. 8–12). The difficulty of making a concise statement was enhanced by the absence of complete agreement on the subject among the members themselves. The volume *Freedom and Fellowship in Religion,* published by the Association (Boston, 1875), collected representative essays by Wasson, Samuel Longfellow, Johnson, Weiss, Potter, Abbot, Frothingham, Chadwick, Higginson, and Ednah D. Cheney designed to display the common assumptions of the leading radicals, as well as their individual peculiarities. The common agreements comprised the substance of free religion, generally speaking. They should have been sifted out and published separately.

Frothingham's writings reflect most accurately the general spirit of the movement. His *Religion of Humanity* (New York, 1872), of which I have been unable to locate a possible earlier edition, may be taken as the representative essay in free religion. His *Recollections and Impressions* (New York, 1891) have a certain retrospective value. Use has also been made of his sermons, nearly all of those preached in the decade of the 1870's having been printed. When Abbot renounced Christianity and

removed to Toledo, Ohio, in 1869, he preached a series of sermons to the
Unitarian society there with the avowed purpose of converting it to the
new faith. These general statements of free religion were printed in *The
Index*, I, nos. 2–5 (January, 1870). The first numbers of *The Index* carried the "Fifty Affirmations," a concise summary in fifty articles of Abbot's version of free religion.

Of the younger theists Chadwick and Savage were also prolific pub-
lishers of sermons. Characteristic statements of their religious ideas were:
J. W. Chadwick, *The Faith of Reason* (Boston, 1879); *Faith on Earth,
and other Sermons* (Boston, 1887); M. J. Savage, *Belief in God: An
Examination of Some Fundamental Theistic Problems* (Boston, 1881);
*Evolution and Religion from the Standpoint of One who Believes in Both*
(Philadelphia, 1886); *Our Unitarian Gospel* (Boston, 1898). As co-editor
of *The Index* from 1880 to 1886 W. J. Potter contributed many articles
to the periodical in that period. A representative summary of free religion from his pen may be found there, n.s., II (January 5, 1882),
317–318.

Emerson's short addresses at the Annual Meetings in 1867 and 1869
expressed the transcendentalist version of free religion. (F.R.A., *Proceedings, 1867*, pp. 52–54; *Proceedings, 1869*, pp. 42–43.) From the point
of view of agnosticism, Felix Adler expressed his agreements and differences with the free religious platform when he resigned from the presidency of the Association in 1882. (*The Index*, n.s., II, June 8, 1882, 606–
607.) Frequent editorials by B. F. Underwood, the materialist, dot the
pages of *The Index* during the years 1880–1886, when Underwood was
co-editor.


CHAPTER V

The items relating to the formation of the Free Religious Association
indicated in Chapter III contain the material for reconstructing its activity. W. J. Potter, *The Free Religious Association, Its Twenty-five Years
and Their Meaning* (Boston, 1892), outlines the early history of the Association.


CHAPTER VI

A useful survey of religious developments after 1865, emphasizing
changes within denominational lines, is W. E. Garrison, *The March of
Faith: the Story of Religion in America Since 1865* (New York and Lon-

don, 1933). The best contemporary treatment of free religion is that of a Belgian, Count E. F. A. Goblet d'Alviella, *The Contemporary Evolution of Religious Thought in England, America, and India,* translated from the French by J. Moden (New York, 1896). Goblet, however, is concerned almost exclusively with the impact of science upon religious liberalism. The popular revolt against Christian orthodoxy in the later nineteenth century has been outlined in R. H. Gabriel, *The Course of American Democratic Thought* (New York, 1940).

For a more detailed account of the Religion of Humanity movement see Sidney Warren, *American Freethought, 1860–1914* (New York, 1943). F. L. Mott, *A History of American Magazines* (3 vols., Cambridge, Mass., 1930–38), in the third volume lists the more important radical religious and popular scientific magazines. References to many others may be found in the exchange columns of any periodical of the time devoted to similar controversial issues. For this purpose the files of *The Index* have been useful in giving hints of the extent of the religious revolt.

The impact of Darwinism upon orthodox religious thinking in America is now beginning to receive the attention it deserves. B. J. Loewenberg, "The Controversy over Evolution in New England," *The New England Quarterly,* VIII (June, 1935), 232–257, was one of the first studies of this subject. At a more systematic level Herbert W. Schneider's "The Influence of Darwin and Spencer on American Philosophical Theology," *Journal of the History of Ideas,* VI (January, 1945), 3–18, is indispensable. Richard Hofstadter's *Social Darwinism in American Thought, 1860–1915* (Philadelphia, 1944) also discusses the reaction of representative Protestant theologians. A study of the new scientific periodicals of the period, such as the *Popular Science Monthly,* will throw much light upon the problem. F. H. Foster, *The Modern Movement in American Theology* (New York, 1939), devotes a chapter to the effects of Darwinism upon Congregationalism and Presbyterianism.

## CHAPTER VII

F. E. Abbot, "The Practical Work of Free Religion," *The Index,* I, no. 6 (February 5, 1870), 2–3, is the best short statement of the social obligations of free religion as the radicals generally conceived them. *The Proceedings at the Second Annual Meeting of the Free Religious Association . . .* (Boston, 1869) contains papers on religion and social reform by Wasson, Henry Blackwell, Lucy Stone, and Rowland Connor. Other materials bearing on free religious reform have been drawn from *The Index* as indicated in the footnotes.

# INDEX

ABBOT, FRANCIS ELLINGWOOD, 17, 40, 44, 47, 55, 97, 112, 131, 155; early career and beliefs, 31–35; attack on transcendentalism, 35–38; scientific theism and free religion, 52–53; attack on Christianity, 60–61; conception of God, 68–69; rejects immortality, 71–72; later career, 84–85; urges active policy, 94–95; fights Christian amendment, 116–117; "Nine Demands of Liberalism," 117–118; the Liberal League, 118–125; on democracy and free speech, 122–123; revised theory of liberalism, 125–129; on social reform, 139–142, 145, 149. *See also Index, The.*

Absolute religion. *See* Parker, Theodore.

Adams, Henry, 56

Adler, Felix, 107, 144, 150; joins F. R. A., 53; his agnosticism, 70–71; proposes policy for F. R. A., 94; resigns presidency, 96

Agassiz, Louis, 111

Agnosticism, 36, 53, 65, 100, 101

Alcott, Bronson, 93

American Social Science Association, 133

American Unitarian Association. *See* Unitarianism, American, denominational organizations.

Andrew, Gov. John A., 14

Association of Liberal Thinkers, 82–83

Atheism, 36; and free religion, 70, 101

BABCOCK, J. M. L., 147–148

Bartol, Cyrus A., career, 25; aids organization of F. R. A., 43–44

Baur, Ferdinand Christian. *See* Tuebingen school of criticism.

Beecher, Henry Ward, 25, 56, 152

Bellows, Henry W., 30, 102; ethical implications of religion, 9–10; interpretation of Scripture, 10; denominational organization, 12–16

Bennett, D. M., 103, 118, 119, 120; for repeal of Comstock laws, 121; controversy with Abbot, 121–124

Blanchard, Henry, on Universalism, 46

Brahmo-Somaj, 78, 80, 91, 91 n

Brown, Olympia, addresses F. R. A., 77

Brownson, Orestes, 52

Burleigh, C. C., 16

Butler, Samuel, 126

Butts, Asa K., 88, 89, 103

CALVINISM, Unitarian break with, 2; harsh doctrines of, 3; on transcendental Unitarianism, 6

Carnegie, Andrew, 135

Centennial Congress of Liberals. *See* National Liberal League.

Chadwick, John White, on rational religion, 62, 63; on immortality, 71. *See also* Cosmism.

Channing, William Ellery (1780–1842), organizes Berry Street Conference of Ministers, 2; on Unitarian orthodoxy, 3, 12; relation to Unitarianism, 4, 8; relation to transcendentalism, 6

Channing, William Henry, addresses F. R. A., 78

"Channing Unitarianism," 14

Cheney, Ednah D., on free religion and reform, 132–133

Chestnut Street Club, 39

Child, Lydia Maria, Channing's letter to, 5

Christern, Mrs. F. W., 89

Christian Amendment movement, 93, 102, 114–116, 116 n

Christian confession, Unitarianism and, 1–2; inconsistent with democracy, 42

Christian socialism, 135

Civil War, as moral crusade, 1

Clarke, James Freeman, 16; at Harvard, 22; defends Christian confession, 40; compromise proposal, 41; addresses F. R. A., 77

Clifford, W. K., 82–83

Cobbe, Frances Power, 81

Coleridge, Samuel Taylor, 81

Collyer, Robert, 25

Comparative religion, and transcendentalism, 23–24; scientific implications, 37; as basis of free religion, 67. *See also* Free religion.